First World War
and Army of Occupation
War Diary
France, Belgium and Germany

2 DIVISION
Divisional Troops
Anti-Aircraft Section
and Divisional Ammunition Column
5 August 1914 - 31 December 1918

WO95/1328

The Naval & Military Press Ltd
www.nmarchive.com
Published in association with The National Archives

Published by

The Naval & Military Press Ltd

Unit 10 Ridgewood Industrial Park,

Uckfield, East Sussex,

TN22 5QE England

Tel: +44 (0) 1825 749494

www.naval-military-press.com

www.nmarchive.com

This diary has been reprinted in facsimile from the original. Any imperfections are inevitably reproduced and the quality may fall short of modern type and cartographic standards.

© Crown Copyright
Images reproduced by permission of The National Archives, London, England, 2015.

Contents

Document type	Place/Title	Date From	Date To
Heading	BEF 2 Div Troops A.A. Section Nov Dec 1914 Disbanded 19/12/14		
Heading	2nd Divisional Anti Aircraft Vol III 1-30.11.14		
War Diary	Eksternest	01/11/1914	04/11/1914
War Diary	1/2 Mile N.W. of Hooge Chateau	05/11/1914	09/11/1914
War Diary	Eksternest	10/11/1914	11/11/1914
War Diary	1/2 Mile N.W. of Hooge Chateau	12/11/1914	12/11/1914
War Diary	Eksternest	13/11/1914	16/11/1914
War Diary	Locre	17/11/1914	18/11/1914
War Diary	Meteren	19/11/1914	30/11/1914
Miscellaneous	2nd Div. L. Anti Aircraft Sect. Vol IV 1-19.12.14		
War Diary	Meteren	01/12/1914	17/12/1914
War Diary	Rouge Croix	18/12/1914	19/12/1914
Miscellaneous	2 Div Ammu. Column		
Miscellaneous	Major Desmond G. Trouton's experiences in the early fighting of 1914.		
Heading	2nd Divisional Royal Artillery 2nd Divl Ammn Column R.F.A. 1914 Aug-1915 Dec		
Heading	2nd Divisional Artillery. 34th Brigade R.F.A. Ammunition Column August 1914		
War Diary	Wassigny	05/08/1914	20/08/1914
War Diary	Givry	23/08/1914	24/08/1914
War Diary	Bavaye	25/08/1914	29/08/1914
War Diary	Amigny	30/08/1914	30/08/1914
Heading	2nd Division XXXIV Bde R.F.A. War Diary XXXIV Brigade Ammunition Column R.F.A. October 1914		
War Diary		01/10/1914	31/10/1914
Heading	2nd Division XXXIV Bde R.F.A. War Diary XXXIV Brigade Ammunition Column R.F.A. November 1914		
War Diary		01/11/1914	30/11/1914
Heading	2nd Division XXXIV Bde R.F.A. War Diary XXXIV Brigade Ammunition Column R.F.A. 3-30th December 1914		
War Diary		03/12/1914	30/12/1914
Miscellaneous	Dvl Ammn Column Aug-Dec 1914		
Diagram etc	Studding Parts For Raised Floor Huts & V Use With Steel Framework Huts Only.		
Heading	2nd Divisional Artillery. 2nd Divisional Ammunition Column R.F.A. January 1915		
War Diary	Robecq	01/01/1915	31/01/1915
Heading	2nd Divisional Artillery. 2nd Divisional Ammunition Column R.F.A. February 1915		
War Diary	Robecq	01/02/1915	03/02/1915
War Diary	Gonnehem	04/02/1915	27/02/1915
War Diary	La Beuvriere	28/02/1915	28/02/1915
Heading	2nd Divisional Artillery. 2nd Divisional Ammunition Column R.F.A. March 1915		
War Diary	La Beuviere	01/03/1915	26/03/1915
War Diary	Fouquereuil	27/03/1915	31/03/1915

Heading	2nd Divisional Artillery. 2nd Divisional Ammunition Column R.F.A. April 1915		
War Diary	Fouquereuil	01/04/1915	24/04/1915
War Diary	Fouquereuil	25/04/1915	30/04/1915
Heading	2nd Divisional Artillery. 2nd Divisional Ammunition Column R.F.A. May 1915		
War Diary	Fouquereuil	01/05/1915	19/05/1915
War Diary	Cornet Malo	20/05/1915	26/05/1915
War Diary	Ames	27/05/1915	31/05/1915
Heading	2nd Divisional Artillery. 2nd Divisional Ammunition Column R.F.A. June 1915		
War Diary	Fouquereuil	01/06/1915	06/06/1915
War Diary	Hesdinguel	07/06/1915	28/06/1915
War Diary	Annezin	29/06/1915	30/06/1915
Heading	2nd Divisional Artillery. 2nd Divisional Ammunition Column R.F.A. July 1915		
War Diary	Annezin	01/07/1915	12/07/1915
War Diary	Oblinghem	13/07/1915	31/07/1915
Heading	2nd Divisional Artillery. 2nd Divisional Ammunition Column R.F.A. August 1915		
War Diary	Oblinghem	01/08/1915	31/08/1915
Heading	2nd Divisional Artillery. 2nd Divisional Ammunition Column R.F.A. September 1915		
War Diary	Oblinghem	01/09/1915	30/09/1915
Heading	2nd Divisional Artillery. 2nd Divisional Ammunition Column R.F.A. October 1915		
War Diary	Oblinghem	01/10/1915	31/10/1915
Heading	2nd Divisional Artillery. 2nd Divisional Ammunition Column R.F.A. November 1915		
War Diary	Oblinghem	01/11/1915	26/11/1915
War Diary	Fouquieres	27/11/1915	30/11/1915
Heading	2nd Divisional Artillery. 2nd Divisional Ammunition Column R.F.A. December 1915		
War Diary	Fouquereuil	01/12/1915	31/12/1915
Heading	2nd Division Divl Artillery. 2nd Divl. Ammn Column R.F.A. Jan-Dec 1916		
Heading	2nd Divisional Artillery. 2nd Divisional Ammunition Column R.F.A. January 1916		
War Diary	Fouquieres	01/01/1916	31/01/1916
Heading	2nd Divisional Artillery. 2nd Divisional Ammunition Column R.F.A. February 1916		
War Diary	Fouquieres	01/02/1916	29/02/1916
Heading	2nd Divisional Artillery. 2nd Divisional Ammunition Column R.F.A. March 1916		
War Diary	Barlin	01/03/1916	23/03/1916
War Diary	Bruay	24/03/1916	31/03/1916
Heading	2nd Divisional Artillery. 2nd Divisional Ammunition Column R.F.A. April 1916		
War Diary	Bruay	01/04/1916	19/04/1916
War Diary	Barlin	20/04/1916	30/04/1916
Heading	2nd Divisional Artillery. 2nd Divisional Ammunition Column R.F.A. May 1916		
War Diary	Barlin	01/05/1916	14/05/1916
War Diary	Bruay	15/05/1916	20/05/1916
War Diary	Caucourt	21/05/1916	21/05/1916
War Diary	Gauchin Legal	22/05/1916	26/05/1916

War Diary	Caucourt	27/05/1916	31/05/1916
Heading	2nd Divisional Artillery. 2nd Divisional Ammunition Column R.F.A. June 1916		
War Diary	Caucourt	01/06/1916	30/06/1916
Heading	War Diary 2nd Divisional Ammunition Column. July 1916		
Miscellaneous	D.A.G. 3rd Echelon Base	31/08/1916	31/08/1916
War Diary	Caucourt	01/07/1916	19/07/1916
War Diary	Moving by Rail	20/07/1916	21/07/1916
War Diary	Caucourt	21/07/1916	21/07/1916
War Diary	Vecquemont Or Douars	22/07/1916	24/07/1916
War Diary	Bois De Tailles Nr. Bray Sur Somme	25/07/1916	25/07/1916
War Diary	Bray	26/07/1916	28/07/1916
War Diary	Near Bray (L.9.a.)	29/07/1916	30/07/1916
War Diary	Meaulte	31/07/1916	31/07/1916
Heading	2nd Divisional Artillery. 2nd Divisional Ammunition Column R.F.A. August And September 1916		
War Diary	Meaulte	01/08/1916	11/08/1916
War Diary	W of Meaulte	12/08/1916	12/08/1916
War Diary	Meaulte	13/08/1916	22/08/1916
War Diary	To Bois De Tailles	23/08/1916	23/08/1916
War Diary	Vecquemont	24/08/1916	24/08/1916
War Diary	Allonville	25/08/1916	25/08/1916
War Diary	Sarton	25/08/1916	27/08/1916
War Diary	Coigneux & St Leger	28/08/1916	29/08/1916
War Diary	Coigneux	30/08/1916	31/08/1916
War Diary	St Leger	01/09/1916	12/09/1916
War Diary	St Leger Les Authie	13/09/1916	30/09/1916
Heading	2nd Divisional Artillery. 2nd Divisional Ammunition Column R.F.A. October 1916		
War Diary	St Leger Les Authie	01/10/1916	03/10/1916
War Diary	Bivouac W Bus.	04/10/1916	07/10/1916
War Diary	Bivouac N.E-Bus	08/10/1916	17/10/1916
War Diary	1/2 Mile NE. of Bus.	18/10/1916	31/10/1916
Heading	2nd Divisional Artillery. 2nd Divisional Ammunition Column R.F.A. December 1916		
War Diary	Bus	01/12/1916	01/12/1916
War Diary	Amplier	02/12/1916	02/12/1916
War Diary	Heirmont	03/12/1916	03/12/1916
War Diary	Froyelles	04/12/1916	06/12/1916
War Diary	Froyelles & Neighbourhood	07/12/1916	25/12/1916
War Diary	Froyelles & District	26/12/1916	31/12/1916
Miscellaneous	2nd Divl. Ammun. Col.		
Heading	2nd Divisional Artillery. 2nd Divisional Ammunition Column R.F.A. November 1916		
War Diary	N.E. of Bus	01/11/1916	05/11/1916
War Diary	Bus	06/11/1916	30/11/1916
Heading	2nd Division Royal Artillery 2nd Divl Ammunition Column. Jan-Dec 1917		
Heading	2nd Divisional Artillery. 2nd Divisional Ammunition Column R.F.A. January 1917		
War Diary	Froyelles	01/01/1917	01/01/1917
War Diary	Occoches	02/01/1917	02/01/1917
War Diary	Marieux & Amplier	03/01/1917	03/01/1917
War Diary	Senlis	04/01/1917	05/01/1917
War Diary	Bouzincourt	06/01/1917	31/01/1917

Heading	2nd Divisional Artillery. 2nd Divisional Ammunition Column R.F.A. February 1917		
War Diary	Bouzincourt	01/02/1917	28/02/1917
Heading	2nd Divisional Artillery. 2nd Divisional Ammunition Column R.F.A. March 1917		
War Diary	Bouzincourt	01/03/1917	18/03/1917
War Diary	Porzcirs	19/03/1917	20/03/1917
War Diary	Bouzincourt	21/03/1917	24/03/1917
War Diary	Puchvillers	25/03/1917	26/03/1917
War Diary	B. Berges	27/03/1917	27/03/1917
War Diary	Veil Hesdin	28/03/1917	31/03/1917
War Diary	Gouy Servins	31/03/1917	31/03/1917
Heading	2nd Divisional Artillery. 2nd Divisional Ammunition Column R.F.A. April 1917		
War Diary	Gouy Servins	01/04/1917	15/04/1917
War Diary	Servins	16/04/1917	17/04/1917
War Diary	St. Catherine	18/04/1917	30/04/1917
Heading	2nd Divisional Artillery. 2nd Divisional Ammunition Column R.F.A. May 1917		
War Diary	St Catherine	01/05/1917	31/05/1917
Heading	2nd Divisional Artillery. 2nd Divisional Ammunition Column R.F.A. June 1917		
War Diary	Madagascar C	01/06/1917	30/06/1917
Heading	2nd Divisional Artillery. 2nd Divisional Ammunition Column R.F.A. July 1917		
War Diary	Madagascar X ur	01/07/1917	02/07/1917
War Diary	Bethune	03/07/1917	03/07/1917
War Diary	Vendin	04/07/1917	16/07/1917
War Diary	Bethune	17/07/1917	31/07/1917
Heading	2nd Divisional Artillery. 2nd Divisional Ammunition Column R.F.A. August 1917		
War Diary	Bethune	01/08/1917	31/08/1917
Heading	2nd Divisional Artillery. 2nd Divisional Ammunition Column R.F.A. September 1917		
War Diary	Bethune	01/09/1917	30/09/1917
Heading	2nd Divisional Artillery. 2nd Divisional Ammunition Column R.F.A. October 1917		
War Diary	Bethune	01/10/1917	07/10/1917
War Diary	Nedon	08/10/1917	17/10/1917
War Diary	Steenbcque	18/10/1917	18/10/1917
War Diary	Steenvoorde	18/10/1917	18/10/1917
War Diary	Vlamertinghe	20/10/1917	31/10/1917
Heading	2nd Divisional Artillery. 2nd Divisional Ammunition Column R.F.A. November 1917		
War Diary	Vlamertinghe	01/11/1917	20/11/1917
War Diary	Walow	21/11/1917	24/11/1917
War Diary	Haplincourt	25/11/1917	26/11/1917
War Diary	Ruyaulcourt	27/11/1917	30/11/1917
Heading	2nd Divisional Artillery. 2nd Divisional Ammunition Column R.F.A. December 1917		
War Diary	Ruyaulcourt	01/12/1917	15/12/1917
War Diary	Haplincourt	16/12/1917	31/12/1917
Heading	2nd Division Divisional Arty. Divisional Ammunition Column. R.F.A. Jan-Dec 1918		
Heading	2nd Divisional Artillery. 2nd Divisional Ammunition Column R.F.A. January 1918		

War Diary	Haplincourt	01/07/1918	26/07/1918
War Diary	Dernancourt	27/07/1918	27/07/1918
War Diary	Meta	28/07/1918	31/07/1918
Heading	2nd Divisional Artillery. 2nd Divisional Ammunition Column R.F.A. February 1918		
War Diary	Coulay	01/02/1918	28/02/1918
Heading	2nd Divisional Artillery. 2nd Divisional Ammunition Column R.F.A. March 1918		
War Diary	Coulay	01/03/1918	13/03/1918
War Diary	Ville Sur Corbie	14/03/1917	22/03/1917
War Diary	Bazentin	23/03/1917	26/03/1917
War Diary	Aucheux	27/03/1917	31/03/1917
Heading	2nd Divisional Artillery. 2nd Divisional Ammunition Column R.F.A. April 1918		
War Diary	Varennes	01/04/1918	05/04/1918
War Diary	Milly	06/04/1918	06/04/1918
War Diary	Berlencourt	07/04/1918	11/04/1918
War Diary	Madagascar	12/04/1918	30/04/1918
Heading	2nd Divisional Artillery. 2nd Divisional Ammunition Column R.F.A. May 1918		
War Diary	Madagascar	01/05/1918	07/05/1918
War Diary	Gouves	08/05/1918	31/05/1918
Heading	2nd Divisional Artillery. 2nd Divisional Ammunition Column R.F.A. June 1918		
War Diary	Gouves	01/06/1918	22/06/1918
War Diary	Gaudiempre	23/06/1918	30/06/1918
Heading	2nd Divisional Artillery. 2nd Divisional Ammunition Column R.F.A. July 1918		
War Diary	Gaudiempre	01/07/1918	31/07/1918
Heading	2nd Divisional Artillery. 2nd Divisional Ammunition Column R.F.A. August 1918		
War Diary	Gaudiempre	01/08/1918	26/08/1918
War Diary	Mouchy	27/08/1918	31/08/1918
Heading	2nd Divisional Artillery. 2nd Divisional Ammunition Column R.F.A. September 1918		
War Diary	Les Quesnoy Farm	01/09/1918	02/09/1918
War Diary	Ervillers	03/09/1918	04/09/1918
War Diary	Vaux Court	05/09/1918	22/09/1918
War Diary	Le Ptealon	22/09/1918	30/09/1918
Heading	2nd Divisional Artillery. 2nd Divisional Ammunition Column R.F.A. October 1918		
War Diary	Havrincourt	01/10/1918	02/10/1918
War Diary	Orival Wood	03/10/1918	11/10/1918
War Diary	Noyelles	12/10/1918	18/10/1918
War Diary	Freston	19/10/1918	22/10/1918
War Diary	St Vaast	23/10/1918	24/10/1918
War Diary	St. Python	25/10/1918	31/10/1918
Heading	2nd Divisional Artillery. 2nd Divisional Ammunition Column R.F.A. November 1918		
War Diary	St. Python	01/11/1918	05/11/1918
War Diary	Rueneuve	06/11/1918	14/11/1918
War Diary	Rueneuve	15/11/1918	20/11/1918
War Diary	Maubeuge	21/11/1918	24/11/1918
War Diary	Esterin to Val	25/11/1918	25/11/1918
War Diary	Fontain Le Veque	26/11/1918	29/11/1918
War Diary	Aiseau	30/11/1918	30/11/1918

Heading	2nd Divisional Artillery. 2nd Divisional Ammunition Column R.F.A. December 1918		
War Diary	Aiseau	01/12/1918	04/12/1918
War Diary	Leseves	05/12/1918	12/12/1918
War Diary	Balgeaboch	13/12/1918	13/12/1918
War Diary	Kalterherberg	14/12/1918	14/12/1918
War Diary	Rollestroich	15/12/1918	18/12/1918
War Diary	Dorf Lenders	19/12/1918	20/12/1918
War Diary	Berkerdorf	21/12/1918	31/12/1918

BEF
2 Div Troops

A.A. Section

Nov Dec 1914

Disbanded 19/12/14

121/2596

2nd Division Anti-Aircraft.

Vol III. 1–30.11.14

WAR DIARY   2nd Divn Anti-Aircraft Secn. R.A.
Ref:- 1/100,000 Map of Belgium (OSTEND sheet)

Place, date, time	Event	Remarks
EKSTERNEST Nov 1st – 4th	Engaged 13 aeroplanes (957 yds) unsuccessfully	On the 3rd/4th Nov, owing to the proximity of numerous heavy field batteries, ~~we were subjected~~ we were subjected to heavy effect we shell fire. It was decided therefore to change position
½ mile N.W of HOOGE Chateau Nov 5th – 9th	Engaged 13 aeroplanes (1006 yds) unsuccessfully	On Oct 8th we were joined by the 1st Divn Anti-Aircraft gun, who took up position within 30 yds. of us. Moral effect was observed for the first time, when we compelled an aeroplane coming directly towards us to "right about turn". This fact on seems to support my suggestion in Appendix I, that a

WAR DIARY   2nd Divn. Anti Aircraft Secn R.A.

Ref:- 1/100000 Map of Belgium (OSTEND sheet)

Place, date, time	Event	Remarks
		a battery of 6 guns, instead of 1 gun, be allotted to each Divn, so that not only would moral affect be ~~obtained~~ established, but possibly a hit obtained.
EKSTERNEST Nov 10th	Nil	Weather unsuitable for aeroplane work
EKSTERNEST Nov 11th	Came under infantry fire due to enemy breaking thro' line held by 1st Corps. Retired 1 mile W. to position held from Nov 5th – 9th	No aeroplanes, due to weather conditions
½ mile N.W of HOOGE Chateau Nov 12th	Nil	No aeroplanes, due to weather conditions

WAR DIARY   2nd Divn. Anti Aircraft Secn RA
Ref:- 1/100,000 Map of Belgium (OSTEND sheet)

Place, date, time	Event	Remarks
EKSTERNEST Nov 13th, 14th	Nil	No aeroplanes, due to weather conditions
EKSTERNEST Nov 15th 16th	Nil	(do)
LOCRE Nov 17th 18th	Relieved at EKSTERNEST by the French & moved to LOCRE with 2nd Divn Arty	
METEREN Nov 19th - 30th	In reserve with 1st Army Corps, for refitting & reinforcements	No hostile aeroplanes appeared over this area.

W Dinke Brockman Lt RHA
O.C. 2nd Divn Anti Aircraft Secn

30.11.14.

121/3907

2nd Div^l Auto Aircraft Sec.

Vol IV. 1 – 19.12.14.

War Diary   2nd Divn Anti Aircraft Secn RA
Ref :— 1/100,000 Map of Belgium (OSTEND sheet).

Place, date, time	Event	Remarks
METEREN Dec 1st – 17th	In reserve with 1st Army Corps, for refitment & reinforcements	No hostile aeroplanes appeared over this area
ROUGE CROIX Dec 18th – 19th	Joined up with 2nd Divnl Ammn. Column & carried out the disbandment of the unit	Officers & men absorbed by the 2nd D.A.C. W Drake Brockman Capt R of A O.C. 2nd Divn A-A Secn 19. xii. 14

Index..................

SUBJECT.

1328

Major Desmond. G. Trouton's experiences
in the early fighting of 1914.

No.	Contents.	Date.
2nd Copy	2 DIV AMMO COLUMN	

Major Desmond G. Trouton's experiences in the early fighting of 1914.

(2nd Lieut. D.G. Trouton went out with No. 3 Section of the 2nd Divisional Amm'n Col. - Lt.-Col. F.T. Ravenhill).

I had very fortunately, as it turned out, joined the Special Reserve of the Royal Field Artillery a few weeks before war was declared in the beginning of August 1914.

I was first of all ordered to Woolwich and three days' later transferred to Aldershot where I took up the duties of an officer in charge of the Details left behind.

I was attached to a section of the Divisional Ammunition Column to assist them in the work of mobilisation.

Now an Ammunition Column is non existant prior to the mobilisation order and consequently the work attached to process of turning it out ready for the field is immensely greater than that in any other unit. The C.O. of this unit utilized me to carry on with the routine work leaving the others free for mobilisation work.

During that time we were all inoculated against Typhoid which was administered in a single dose as time was too short for the usual procedure. I was very bad the next day as the heat at that time was very severe for England and as we were all working against time and could not be spared my first experience of soldiering was in a rough school.

On Saturday morning I was sent for by the Adjutant who told me that I might be needed for one of the other sections as they were short of an officer and to get my things in readiness. I sallied out into the town and bought all the service kit available and wired home to town for the rest.

That evening I got the expected orders and after saying good-bye I drove over to Melbrech in a taxi where I spent the night and next morning Dorothy Donald left me at Borden.

I then met Capt. Dresser my new C.O., who told me

Quiller-Couch was the other Sub., so I felt I had at last dropped among friends. I heard at the same time that there was no time to be lost, in fact we sailed on the following Monday night.

I spent the morning making the acquaintance of the N.C.O's, procuring a batman, Gnr. Scott, and a charger, a little black mare.

That was one of the luckiest mornings' I ever had as both Scott and the mare became devoted friends later on; were absolutely paragons.

Time flew as there was so much to do and we were parading for our final march out into the unknown future before one could realize that the hour had come. There is only one incident worth mentioning and that was in mess on Sunday night, when we all drank the Gunner toast of "Fat targets and straight shooting" to the batteries of the 41st Brigade which marched out that night. This was the brigade that blew back the Prussian Guards from the muzzles of their guns on the memorable 11th November when our line was broken for a short time in the first battle of Ypres. If ever a wish came true that toast did.

Monday 17th.

Of our march to the station and the trouble we had with the untrained horses I will say nothing, we got there and were very thankful. We also got on to the ship without serious trouble and very soon found ourselves sailing out into the channel. We reached Havre at daybreak next morning having crossed between continuous lines of destroyers who kept a broad belt across the channel free from any enemy vessel. When I came on deck I found that we were racing another transport for first place in the river. We ran side by side past the ever narrowing banks till you could nearly have jumped from one boat to another. The men on both ships were in the greatest spirits and we joined together in singing every popular song of the moment "Tipperary" included. We retired to breakfast after we had won the race and were very disappointed to

Tuesday 18th.

Wed. 19th.

find the whole river covered in mist when we came on deck again as we had been filled up with stories of the beauty of the river by the genial skipper.

Later on it cleared a bit and we had our first taste of French hospitality from the villagers who lined the banks cheering and singing our National Anthem, when we tried to sing the Mareillaise in return it was rather a failure at first. Soon after lunch we got to Rouen and started to disembark as soon as we were wharfed. It was rather slow as there were not the same facilities for disembarking as in England.

We got away finally and spent the night in the huge rest camp that had sprung up on the outskirts of the town. Next day we met the other sections and the Colonel made a speech to all the officers of the combined column.

Thursday 20th.
We all left next evening and found entraining wagons on the French trucks very different from the end loading in England. However the men worked like heroes and at last we were all on and started on our journey towards the Germans and Berlin as we then thought.

Friday 21st.
We had all night and next day in the train and finally reached our detraining station Landrecies about 3 p.m., next afternoon.

We got out pretty quickly and had orders to spend the night there and move up after the army next day.

Saturday 22nd.
I was sent on ahead next day to find the rest of the column and get orders. I found   deserted so had to push on to Maubeuge where I found that 2nd Div. H.Q'rs were just moving on to a place 10 miles north on the Mons road. As I had already done about 16 miles I tried to get a wire through for orders. While waiting I watered and fed the mare and had lunch myself in the adjoining hotel. After lunch I found most of the headquarters gone and not much hope of getting an answer and until one of the clerks remembered an old message relating to the D.A.C., I was in rather a quandary. He soon

4

found it in the waste paper basket and luckily it gave the position for the D.A.C. for that night.

As I had now got what I wanted I started back and found the Section about 6 miles short of Maubeuge. They were all talking about a "Zep" they had just seen brought down away to the south and I saw smoke rising from where it had fallen.

We were not far from the place mentioned and by striking northwards through bye-roads were soon there and in bivouac for the night.

I had been very interested during the day by the preparations the French were making for the defence of Maubeuge, chiefly barbed wire. Subsequent events showed that deep trenches and dug-outs would have been more to the purpose.

There was a lot of work being done all over the country by civilian labour gangs in putting up barbed wire and levelling trees to improve fields of fire and for making barricades.

As it happened all the work was wasted as we retired rapidly across this ground and held the line through Landrecies.

Sunday 23rd.

Early next morning the rest of the Column came in from the north and we joined them in an orchard near our bivouacs where we all stood in readiness to move at a moment's notice.

Here we heard of the fight of the previous day and saw our first of the effect of shell fire; a gun hit in the fight being sent back to us on its way to the base. The only two survivors of the detachment filled us with stories of the fight but always kept coming back to poor Bill the layer and showed again and again the hole in the seat made by the case which had first passed through Bill. They seemed a bit dazed by it all and certainly that gun with the still fresh/blood marks of brought it home to us all for the first time.

Tuesday 25th Aug.

At about 9 a.m., we got the expected orders and moved to a place just north of Leval where we had lunch. Here we first came across the difficulties of watering 800 horses at one spot, one of the chief items of our daily life and thought for the future. Quiller-Couch was a master hand at this and we came off best that time but on other occasions we were not always so lucky. I was in charge of the Mess and after lunch I procured a hen from an old lady near by who also gave us some most excellent .

In the afternoon we were off again and moved through Leval to another field just south of Landrecies, where we got ready to spend the night.

Many of us got a wash in a stream near by and jolly glad we were after two such hot days and our first night in the open.

But the fates were not done with us yet and we were turned out again at about 6 to move to Le Grand Fayt about 4 miles due east.

When approaching this place we had our first excitement. A few shots were heard in rear and word was passed up for the gunners to fall back as a rear guard. No sooner had these gone, under Quiller, than a couple of shots passed over the wagon I was riding behind. I got hold of three men and got out on that flank on the only hedge coming near the road. On of my men said he saw a man at the hedge but at that moment a line of infantry came out from the village and advancing in open order covered our flank from any more trouble. By this time it was nearly dark and I found to my horror that the section with my horse were going on at the trot so I and the men had to sprint for the last wagon on which we jumped exhausted. I there learned a lesson I never forgot. Never dismount when you are with mounted troops without keeping your horse and a horseholder with you. And many a time has that saved me a two or three mile run.

We came into a field in the centre of the village passing through the cordon of infantry which was drawn round it. There was considerable confusion already and our hasty entry did not lessen it, one man evidently thought us to be

Uhlans as he stuck his bayonet through the leg of one of Quiller's drivers. Soon the rear guard arrived very breathless but triumphant and as most of them knew nothing about a rifle being reservists they began investigating. We had to make them unload as one shot went too near Quiller's head to be comfortable. Things quickly quieted down then except for a heavy battery in the next field which kept banging away into the dark. A cold drizzle started then and we spent a miserable night getting what shelter we could from the wagons and warmth by crowding together.

Wed. 26th Aug. We moved off at daybreak and struck the Landrecies Etreux road road about 5 miles south of Landrecies turning south then to Etreux where we arrived about noon. The early part of this march was exciting as we had our decks cleared for action metaphorically speaking. I gathered that some Uhlans had been located to the south of us, in fact one was pointed out to me about a mile distant by a machine gun officer who was acting as a flank guard to the column. But nothing came of it all and we reached Etreux safely in bright sunlight which dried us after the wet night.

We lunched here and spent a lazy afternoon getting some sleep. Our bivouac was on the high ground to the South of the town and in the evening we watched some heavy guns coming into action on the ridge to the north of the town. We heard about the fight of the Guards at Landrecies the night before and all were wondering what the meaning of this retiring was when on every occasion the men concerned said that they beat the Germans. Rumours of all kinds flew about with lightning speed; one of the most persistent ones was that the Germans had pushed in between us and the 2nd Corps at Le Cateau about 15 miles west of us. This one was so persistent that the Veterinary officer rode off in that direction going out 4 or 5 miles but came back saying that there was nothing there.

Thurs
27th Aug

We were off again at dawn the next morning and by eleven we were bivouaced again on the side of the road. Water was a difficulty here a marsh being the only available source. I remember it was down at the bottom of a six foot bank and our horse nearly mad with thirst from the dust on the roads came slithering down the bank and floundered into the mud. We had an awful job getting him out and in the end got about 40 men on to a rope and pulled him up by main force. Here again we had a slack afternoon but at about 5 we were just finishing a second water when we had to stand to and got orders to move soon after. Our section was to be left behind as the 41st Bde. Ammn. Col. was temporarily lost and the brigade were coming into action about ½ mile back along the road and wanted a reserve.

We moved to a sheltered spot more directly behind them and spent the night ready to stand to at a minute's notice. We were off before dawn and soon rejoined the rest of the Column as they were moving off from where they had spent the night.

28th Aug.

We passed La Fere next day and the next break we had in the monotony of the march, of getting off at daylight with a stop at mid-day and then on again till dark, occurred at Villers-Cotterets. We came into the woods soon after passing La Fere and making our way south we finally approached Villers-Cotterets from the east coming into the wonderful cathedral of trees which seems to be art right into the centre of the Forest just as the rising sun shone down the centre, lighting up the trees with a soft pink effect. To me it seemed so strange to pass through this beautiful country just a day ahead of the Germans and all that their coming must mean. This leads me to speak of the refugees which I have left out so far, to make the thread of the narrative clearer.

From the moment we started the backward move the natives came with us. Even when passing through Leval, a few hours after we had started on our long retreat; we noticed an enormous difference to the appearance of the day before. Many houses were closed and shuttered and carts, prams and every other available vehicle were being hastily loaded with valuables. We left them and passed on but everywhere we came we saw the same thing, the streets being lined with people asking why. Why should England retire, what is the meaning, and next, what are we to do ? But one of the things that all of us noticed was the wonderful welcome we got everywhere and the simple faith these poor people had in the power of the British to protect them. Later on when I/was again in France nearly two years later, I was sorry to see this had largely disappeared and very often the British troops were treated as an unavoidable nuisance. But to get back to the early days, everybody who could gave us something if only a drink of water which I am not sure was not the most acceptable gift of all as the weather was nearly tropical and the dust on the roads dried up the throat till one could hardly swallow. Nothing was too good for the men. Bread, eggs, wine, cider, fruit of all sorts, cigarettes, matches, milk and finally the cool water from the depths of some shady well were among the most frequent presents. I have seen a man well on in years rush into a tobacconists and come out with his hands full of cigarettes soon distributed among the passing men who laughed and thanked and said "Vive la France" and all were happy. And yet all the time these people were getting ready to fly, this greeting was nearly their last act before leaving, as many towns were deserted when the Batteries half a day after us passed through.

      Another form of generosity that I think shows the spirit of France as much as anything was the way these small farmers when leaving their homes with what valuables and stock they could take with them, would willingly give chickens and anything they could to us and would often take no money saying "it is better you should have it than the Bosche".

How they hated the Bosche !   To us it seemed rather ludicrous their earnestness. The old men as we passed would draw their hand across their throat and then make a stabbing movement, calling out some curse on the hated Hun.

The whole matter of the refugees was often comic in spite of the intense tragedy of it all. To see a huge farm cart drawn by a huge ~~a huge~~ Flemish stallion a milch cow and a dog no matter under what circumstances makes you smile and yet perhaps there were two or three families on top with the old grandmothers and hoards of children, the younger women leading the whole along, tramping sturdily beside, sometimes taking their turn for a lift. Many curious collections used to be piled on top of the carts, the Family bed was one of the favourite things in spite of its bulk.

Then on the other hand there were those who had no vehicle at all, these used to generally collect into bands of about 100 and trudge along the road together. It was pathetic to see the children dragging themselves along, but they were all very ~~thankful~~ thoughtful for the weak ones, and our men used also to take the children from the arms of the tired mother or elder sister and put them on to the wagons and often the mother too, although this meant that they themselves had to walk as we could not load up the horses any more than necessary. This was no slight thing as it meant a walk of thirty miles for the man himself.

But the saddest part of all was when the number of refugees on the road threatened to block the army and they had to be turned on to side roads. I was detailed to do this one afternoon of the later days and hated every minute of it. I had to turn the stream off the main road on to a side road which lead on to another parrallel road to us but made a good big round and I found the best way was to tell them this way was shorter, some used to plead tearfully and some with anger but I had a guard and they had to go; many saw how tired I was and just went on without any arguing.

Two girls I remember argued for over half an hour, they tried every means in their power to try and get past, so in the end I handed them over to the Corporal who could not speak French but cleared them down the other road amid roars of laughter. These girls were typical of a large group who took it all as a great joke and were much less trouble to deal with than those who burst into floods of tears and asked you if the germans were close behind, what they had better do, and innumerable other questions which you could not answer. But on the whole they did what they were told without a murmur. I wonder would English refugees be as amenable and what would have happened if they had not obeyed as the guard had loaded rifles and I had orders to let no one pass on any account. I suppose a shot over their heads would have brought them to their senses.

While I am talking on this subject I must mention one woman who stood looking down the road along which we were coming with such a look of unutterable sadness that at the time I longed to be able to put that look on canvas as it seemed to me to contain all that the womanhood of France was passing through with their men in the unknown and their houses about to be destroyed. She stood unmoving looking into the far distance and her face seemed to me to contain all the sadness of the motherhood and wifehood of France in that one strained look.

But to get back to my story we reached Villers-Cotterets early in the morning and had great difficulty in getting water for the horses but in the end got the fire hydrant in a wood factory going and kept some tubs filled where we could water the horses satisfactorily. Towards evening we got orders that half the wagons were to be emptied at the station and sent back to carry the packs of the Infantry. Quiller-Couch was sent with the wagons of all the four sections and we did not see him for 5 days during which time he was roaming round on his own and had many interesting experiences.

The rest of the retreat was uneventful except for

the minor details of the march such as horses casting shoes or galling, and occasionally we had to shoot one that was too done to come any further with us.

Before I start on the term back across the Marne and the subsequent advance to the Aisne I will tell a little of our method of living.

We lived very differently from a mess as known in the subsequent stages of the war. We were travelling light, in fact we were down to our 35 pounds. A valise, a sleeping bag, a change of clothes and linen, our washing things and a burberry was roughly our kit. Our mess kit was very simple, a knife, fork and spoon, a mug and two plates each and plates for the food. We nearly always had stew when we had hot food and had plenty of vegetables as we just helped ourselves in passing. We bought bread, butter, eggs and chickens which we had when we had time to cook them. We generally only had one hot meal a day at about 4 p.m., and used to eat chocolate in the early morning when starting, have some cold bacon and bread or bully and bread at breakfast time and then a hot meal in the evening when we got in, and we used to sleep when we were doing nothing else.

Getting into camp became a matter of a few minutes and moving out quicker. We have all been asleep in an hour and half after turning into the field having watered and fed the horses, cooked our daily meal and washed. And later on we used to allow three quarters of an hour after reveille before marching out, all the harnessing and hooking in being done in the dark. In fact during those days we developed from a collection of novices into a fairly efficient body although we never got the smartness and discipline of regulars.

Sept 6th

Quiller-Couch rejoined us just before the turn came. That turn it sounds a little thing to march back along the road you came the day before but I can't say what it meant to us. We heard nothing only on marching out of the field we turned to the right instead of the left as we had expected and found ourselves going towards the germans. It took some time before the significance sunk in and then the joy; all were laughing, they could not help themselves and all tiredness was forgotten, we seemed to have become a new lot, everything was done with a will and nothing was too much.

Up to this time we as an Ammunition Column had not been used as we were such a huge and unwieldy thing on the road that we were bundled on out of the way as fast as possible so as not to block the road for others. We officers used often to talk about this and Captain Dresser said that if he never saw any more fighting than this he was going to pretend he was not out, and we were quite of the same opinion. We need not have worried as we all got our turn later but somehow those first men did the most wonderful thing of all. A rear guard action of 200 miles in ten days without ever losing touch with the enemy, always turning on him and hurling him back in confusion, seems to me the most wonderful feat of all times when we remember the difference in numbers.

At the time I heard it estimated that the germans had 100,000 casualties during the fighting to the Aisne and our total number was not more than that. We I believe lost 23,000.

Sept 9th

The first couple of days forward were very similar to the earlier days and I myself did not see any fighting till after the Marne was crossed when I was sent on with ammunition to replenish them after the battle. I got up with the army in the evening and got my wagons well caught in the block of traffic at the top of the long hill on the north side of the river. I rode on ahead to find the Bde. Ammn. Col. for which I was bound and met some gunner officers I knew. One of them told me a lot about the fight. How his battery had had to leave the guns owing to the amount of german shell coming over, and how Major, Sergeant Major and he had gone back later and got one gun into action at the retreating germans. What pleased him most was that he had pulled the trigger and wiped out so many himself. I only saw solid masses of Germans retreating over the hills in the distance accompanied by white puffs of shrapnel. I then went back to my wagons having heard my destination and after a long time got them up to the field where the whole brigade was bivouaced with the best part of the rest of the 2nd Division. It was dark when I got there and spent the night with the Ammn. Col. who gave us a share of their meal.

Sept 10th

Next day I had to wait behind to refil from the lorries and got orders from the Colonel where to rejoin as he passed on with the rest of the Column. I had to wait some time and when I finally got off it was afternoon. However I got along and got on to the road leading to this place. The whole road for miles forward and backwards was packed and I found that I was in the middle of the 5th Division. However I was on the right road and they were bound for the same place so I left my wagons in the line and pushed on ahead which turned out to be very lucky as when I got to the village I not only found no signs of the 2nd Div, Ammn. Column but heard that the 2nd Divn. was about 15 miles to the east. I also learned that this village was our outpost line; certainly no place for General Service Wagons. So I hurried back and was able to turn them off into a field about 2 miles back along the road. It was pitch dark by this time and the last wagon was badly driven in at the gate and got one wheel into a deep ditch. Do what we liked we could not get it out and had to unload it and reload after we had got it clear. By this time rain had come on and it was bitterly bitterly cold; we had no food as we had expected to be back with

the rest by then. So I gave the order for half the
emergency rations to be used and we had some hay ready
out in the field for the horses. Soon we had all fed
and turned in for a few hours rest. We started off at
1 a.m., next morning so as to get clear of the 5th Division
before it started, and as soon as we were clear made our way
along a main road running due east. We stopped for breakfast in a village after we had done about 12 miles, and
there I had rather an amusing experience.

I was hunting round the village for bread when a
very excited native came up and told us of a german with
a gun, whose presence had got them into a state of
panic. We drew our revolvers and set out to capture him
with four men, expecting a desperate villain. Our guide
led us to a large house with a red cross flag and then
pointed us on ahead. We entered the courtyard with
caution, found it empty, the guide then followed us and
pointed to a french window "in there, in there" he kept
repeating. We quickly entered the room ready for anything
and found ourselves in a sick ward with about a dozen
cases, nothing else, so we hauled in the man and he pointed
to one of the cases. This man turned out to be a german
who had gone to bed. He had tied a huge bandage round a
cut in his arm and pretended to be badly wounded. I
think he had hit on this plan as the safest way to surrender,
anyway he had given this old man and his wife an awful
fright, the night before, when he had arrived and demanded
admittance. We soon had him out of bed and made him dress.
One of the men found his rifle under his matress so we
brought him along with us. I got the badge of his helmet
as a souvenir of such an amusing incident.

After breakfast we pushed on and found the rest
still in camp though about to start in an hour's time.
It turned out that they had had their marching orders
changed after they had left us and had left an orderly

to redirect us but he had got tired of waiting and had come on without us; hence our little pilgrimage.

The remainder of the advance to the Aisne was without special incident, and two days later we found ourselves on the plateau between Braisne and Bourg, where we were destined to remain for many a long day.

Up to this time we had never spent more than one night in any place so that here we entered into quite a different phase in the fighting. The first night we spent at the top of the long hill above Braisne, having got into our bivouac after dark. Early next morning we were up and moved along the road towards Bourg but only for a short distance, where we waited in a field beside the road. Here we saw shrapnel at close hand for the first time. A couple of batteries were in action about 500 to 800 yards north of us and the germans were trying to get on to them. They put most of the "stuff" over, some rounds coming fairly close to us, so we were moved along the road to a safer spot. We spent most of the day there without any incident. Quiller and I went across the road and over the fields till we could see down into the valley of the Aisne and there I saw a battle field for the first time. My first impression was acute disappointment. I had expected to see something exciting going on, instead everything seemed normal, but presently one began to pick out little things that a trained eye would have seen at once. Little puffs of white smoke which quickly dissolved in the breeze, gradually obtruded themselves on your notice and by using field glasses you could catch glimpses of the moving troops. Some wagons in the bottom of the valley carefully drawn up behind a line of trees, occasionally a little line of men would appear for a moment, advance and disappear again as suddenly as it appeared, but the whole impression was of a deserted countryside, except for the noise which had first drawn us there in expectation. This noise is a sound that once heard is never forgotten. The boom of the guns and the occasional shriek of a shell are the sounds that first obtrude themselves to the ear, but presently the continuous rumble or rather crackle of musketry seems to dominate all. This is one of the most fascinating sounds imaginable, in the distance it is like the sound of a bright log fire on a frosty night; suddenly quickening up and then dying away again to burst out once more in waves of sound. I have often lain awake during a night attack in the distance, listening to it gradually growing up then dying away, only to flare up more loudly, ever increasing in volume till the guns begin to speak, first one and then more and more as the fight thickens till the maximum intensity is reached with a roar of sound as the machine guns rattle out their stream of lead, and then suddenly silence; another attack has failed. One shot followed by two or three, then a little burst of fire and all is over for that time, quiet again reigns and back to the land of "nod".

However we could not stop watching for long and had to get back to the section where we then lunched but were unable to water the horses. Suddenly we had the stand to, and at the same moment a broken line of infantry straggled back over the spot we had been watching the fight from. We began moving out and back along the road with orders to put out a flank guard on our right. There was no need to bustle the tired men, the stories of the infantry who had joined us was sufficient, they jumped and we were quickly back in our former position. I remember a machine gun belonging to them was put into action on the rear wagon as the gun detachment expected the germans over the ridge at any moment. It was the first

17

real panic I had ever seen; this company had got caught by a large number of machine guns and had been very badly cut up and these men had come the whole way back thinking they were followed by the germans. They had lost all their officers and N.C.O's, whether knocked out or left behind I never heard, but the men were quickly collected and went back again under a P.M., who turned up. I always felt sorry for those fellows, they were done to the world with the last few weeks hard work and undoubtedly had been very roughly handled; very few could not show a hole in their clothing and a lot had minor cuts on some part of their bodies. They got very little sympathy and got a pretty good dressing down, but at that time local panics like that might have serious results and were very quickly sat on. It was the only case I have ever come across and was of course due to there being nobody to take charge. I felt sicker than ever at being in an Ammunition Column after that, where like a hare you have to run at the first sign of danger, as it would be impossible to do anything with a line of wagons over a mile long with about eighty untrained riflemen to defend it.

So when we had been there for about a week you can imagine our joy when we heard that all the subalterns were going to be sent up to the Brigade Ammunition Columns to replace the officers there who had been drafted into the batteries to fill up casualties. So that my time with the Divisional Ammunition Columns practically coincided with the moving fighting and I spent the best part of this first spell of trench fighting in the Brigade Amm'n Column.

I think I better break the narrative at this time to explain the composition of the Artillery and Ammunition supply of a division. In a division, this does not hold now as things have been altered to fit new conditions, there were four brigades of artillery each containing three 6 gun batteries. Three brigades consisted of 18 pdr Field guns and the fourth of 4.5" Howitzers. In addition there was one battery of Heavys, composed of four 60 pdr guns. In each battery there were two limbered ammunition wagons for each gun as well as the ammunition carried in the gun limbers. Thus each brigade had an ammunition column of its own which had one limbered ammunition wagon for each gun of the brigade, making 18 wagons. It also had 7 small-arm carts and two G.S. wagons (General Service) for supplying the infantry. Each infantry brigade is attached to an artillery brigade for ammunition supply and are worked together as much as possible for this reason. Thus we have the four Brigade ammunition columns who in turn are supplied by the Divisional column which is composed of four sections, three carrying 18 pdr ammunition and small-arm, while the fourth supplies the howitzers and heavies. Each section contains 28 G.S. wagons which are drawn by six horse teams, so that the whole column is much bigger than an entire brigade of artillery including its own column. The Divisional Column is supplied by motor lorries from the Ammunition Park at rail head.

Well I had now joined the 41st Brigade and was in part of a combatant unit and although we did no fighting it was no rare thing for us to get under fire. I joined the unit when it was just camped beside the canal on the east side of Bourg. By this time we had given up trying to push the Germans any further and were ourselves again on the defensive and I remember on my first afternoon watching the 'Jack Johnsons' bursting round a french battery on a spur to the north-east of us. We had never imagined anything so big then and watched the sight of cottages going skywards with a kind of incredulous fascination. I must now describe the unit I had joined. Capt. Thornton was O.C.; he was an ideal soldier to work under for a beginner like me. He demanded the best of everybody and got it, saying very little the whole time. He did most things by fixed rules which everyone knew and there was never any doubt about what to do in consequence. I dont think he was very pleased when he first got me, he had just lost two regular subalterns, and I was a very poor substitute with all my inexperience. However I soon settled down and he left me most of the routine work when once he had explained all his methods. He was one of the finest of horse masters and never left anything undone that might help the beasts, with the result that he had the finest lot of horses in the division as certified by both the C.R.A., and the A.D.V.S., when they came round on their inspections. There was a great difference in the discipline of the whole unit to that in the one I had left. For all the N.C.O's were regulars and also nearly half the men, the rest being old soldiers of the reserve, and this had given them much more chance of settling down to a proper state of things that we had had when our Sergeant Major had been a reserve corporal and the rest had been picked from the ranks.

When I joined the unit I found that a neighbouring straw stack had been raided and all the horses were standing in a foot of bedding thus getting very much better rest at night. Even then after that short rest all but a few looked in the pink of condition and this was explained to me by the superior march discipline Thornton had organized. He had it as a standing rule that at every stop all the horses were to be watered without any orders if there was water within 100 yards, and consequently the horses got many drinks during the day and could be given plenty of time for feeding during the mid-day halt, when most people had to start by watering and then had to move on before the horses were half finished with their oats. He was also extremely particular about the grooming which was as thorough as in barracks, and he used to spend an hour himself every morning vetting all the sick horses and looking out for any thin ones who needed extra food or rest.

The 41st Brigade was in reserve if its position can be called reserve, as the guns were in action and constantly used, but they were on the hills to the south of the Aisne while the rest of the Divisional Artillery was on the northern bank of the river. Now all the Brigade ammunition columns were collected in the flat stretch of land on the south of the canal so that we had to go back to supply the batteries. It seemed a silly state of affairs but it enabled us to give the horses a little draught exercise thus keeping them used to the work. The first trouble we had came very soon; one day while going along the road to Pont D'Arcy on the way to the batteries, a sudden screech and bang; a shell burst right above the head of the column scattering its bullets well over. I was behind but soon had them trotting out round the corner into the woods and safety, but they got in a second round at us just before the rear was away, one shell bursting on each side of us. One of the horses shied and the driver who was equally frightened left go, so I and the sergeant stopped to catch it for him to have the pleasure of another salvo on each side of us. But we all got away without a scratch and for ever after avoided that corner which later on became locally known as "dead man's "corner". That road then being shut we had to find other ways. For the next few days we came up and down a parrallel valley to the east but the germans got on to the road just above the village where there was ah open bit and that became unhealthy.

So later I got a way where by starting up the eastern valley and then cutting round the shoulder of the hill into the other valley through the woods we were only visible for a few yards. This worked alright for a couple of days but coming back just before lunch one day we no sooner brought the first wagon down a bank into the open bit ~~that~~ than "bang, bang" they dropped a couple of rounds about 200 yards short. I did not wait for the next round but trotted out till we were well clear and then halted for a bit to throw them out with their timing. We had the pleasure of watching them shell the spot where we joined the main road at the time they thought us due and when they had finished we went home.

Next afternoon was exciting, we had made our trip without any excitement and were resting when we saw some horses being shelled at dead man's corner. The horses bolted and the bulk made for our camp which was best part of a mile off so we had plenty of time to get the men to our horses heads. We caught the horses, they were glad of any protection, and were looking at their wounds, most were dripping with blood when I noticed that the german shells were following them into our camp. I gave the order to file out of camp and the men were just filing out when a six gun salvo burst right over the spot where I had the N.C.O's collected for instructions. I had a very narrow shave the fuse of one shell landing just beside my foot and the man on either side being hit. I saw the Sergeant Major go flat on his face but found him later perfectly fit and looking after the two wounded who were the only casualties besides Sergeant Smith who was killed on the spot. We were very lucky to get off as well as we did as the whole lot of us were in the danger zone which I afterwards examined and found that there were bullet marks in every yard of the area. I quickly got the men and horses clear of the camp and away to the woods and sent a ~~message~~ messenger for stretchers for the wounded men who were under cover of the wagons, and then I had to see to the horses. One was down and nearly dead and another had lost a foot so I had to shoot them as well as another who was badly hit about the head and was perceptibly dying. They put over a few more rounds but we were able to shelter behind the wagons and had no more trouble. I then went over to the rest and got them back from the front edge of the wood just in time as the Germans began searching it almost as soon as we were clear. After dark we came back to camp and next day moved to a place on the hills behind very near where I had been with the Divisional Ammn. Col. This was the first time I had ever had a near shave and made a great impression on me although I have since been in worse corners. We were very lucky to get off so lightly with men although we had 18 horses hit, thirteen of which subsequently died. I put this down to the fact that the men were leading their horses out and were sheltered between the two animals.

This makes it sound as if we were having a bad time but we were there for a fortnight altogether and that was all the trouble we had. I had great times on the whole and used to be out riding on my own a lot. We had the small arm carts with the H.Q. of the Guards Brigade whom we supplied and I used to often visit them on the days when the Captain did not. I got to know all the country round very well and enjoyed my time there more than any other I can remember.

-x-x-x-x-

2ND DIVISION
ROYAL ARTILLERY

2ND DIVL AMMN COLUMN R.F.A.

1914 AUG — 1915 DEC

2nd Divisional Artillery.

34th BRIGADE R. F. A. AMMUNITION COLUMN

AUGUST 1914.

WAR DIARY or INTELLIGENCE SUMMARY

Army Form C. 2118.

Hour, Date, Place	Summary of Events and Information	Remarks and references to Appendices
WAUDONY Aug 5th 1914 / Aug 20th	Mobilised. Brigade advanced for concentration of 2nd Div. Division in a place close to Belgian frontier.	
GIVRY Aug 23rd	20th & 37th Batty in action near VILLE REUILLE "LE GAZ". 22nd Batty in a support E. of GIVRY. 50th & 70th subject to heavy shell-fire in the afternoon. their mobile howitzer Batts turned on them, troops however maintained their fire. L/S Retroullett + Bussard wounded. 3 NCOs men Killed. 27 wounded	
	Aug 24th. During night 20th Batty, which had had three guns damaged, was withdrawn. 22nd moved up into action under same ways but went to S.W. flank. 50th & 47th How. Batty (one 13 Pdr) which had been sent up during the night joined the Bde + came into action in left of 22nd. Liability by the indestigant withdrawal of our position. All about 9 am a stampede was opened from the right by the Rifle Brigade. The Bde received fresh orders from Brigade 22nd Batty in action with Rear Guard (6th Inf Bde)	
BAVAY Aug 25th / Aug 26th-29th	Retirement via SAMBRE and to AMIGNY. Bde on rearguard with 5th Inf Bde at Pont-sur-SAMBRE	
AMIGNY Aug 31st	Position occupied covering crossings of river	

2nd Division
XXXIV Bde R.F.A.

WAR DIARY

XXXIV BRIGADE AMMUNITION COLUMN

R. F. A.

October

1914

34th Bde R.F.A.

WAR DIARY
or
INTELLIGENCE SUMMARY.
(Erase heading not required.)

Army Form C. 2118.

October 1914.

Hour, Date, Place	Summary of Events and Information	Remarks and references to Appendices
October 1st	In Camp at BOURG. Small arm carts formed an advanced Echelon at SOUPIR with Infantry 1st line transport. 18 Pr Ammunition supplied direct to Firing Battery wagons.	J.W.R.
1 p.m. October 6th	Received orders to move at 7 p.m.	
7 p.m.	Moved to BRAINE accompanied by a section of the 44th Bde Amm Col. Our small arm carts cleared up traffic. Parked wagons under cover along Rue de REMPARTS. Horses stabled in sheds. Officers billeted Chateau with 50th Battery.	J.W.R.
October 7th	22nd and 70th Batteries in action behind ridge W. of BRENELLE. Ammunition supply possible only by day on account of woods. Ordered up 6 April 16 Pr Infantry Bde at VAILLY with S.A.A. On getting touch with them in the morning, found that they did not require any ammunition. They arranged to let us know if they wanted any as they had large quantities on the ground.	J.W.R.

Army Form C. 2118.

WAR DIARY
or
INTELLIGENCE SUMMARY.
(Erase heading not required.)

October

Instructions regarding War Diaries and Intelligence Summaries are contained in F.S. Regs., Part II. and the Staff Manual respectively. Title pages will be prepared in manuscript.

Hour, Date, Place	Summary of Events and Information	Remarks and references to Appendices
4 p.m. Oct 12	Received orders to move at 6 p.m. to LOUPEIGNE	
6 p.m. "	Moved. Arrived at about 8.30 p.m. Bivouaced around a wood by the side of the road. Ordered to march at 6 a.m. to FERE EN TARDENOIS to entrain. Road good.	J.U.R.
6 a.m. Oct 13	Marched FERE EN TARDENOIS. Started entraining at 10.15 a.m. completed at 11 a.m. Went via PARIS to CALAIS.	J.U.R.
Oct 14	Passing through CALAIS arrived at SAINT OMER	
12 Midday "	Started to detrain.	
2.30 p.m. "	Left station.	J.U.R.
4.30 p.m. "	Marched to Cavalry Barracks and billeted for the night with the 34th Brigade.	
October 15	Marched with 34th Bde to CERCUS & returned in School.	J.U.R.
October 17.	Marched with the Brigade to STEEN VOORDE and billeted in a farm.	J.U.R.

WAR DIARY or INTELLIGENCE SUMMARY.

Army Form C. 2118.

October

Hour, Date, Place	Summary of Events and Information	Remarks and references to Appendices
2.30 a.m. October 19.	Received orders to join 2nd Division at GODEWAERSVELDE at 9 a.m.	
6 a.m. "	Moved off from STEENVOORDE and marched via GODEWAERSVELDE (where we joined the Division) BOESCHEPE & RENINGHELST to a Château on North side of YPRES - VLAMERTINGHE road at the level crossing. Billeted in the Château, Roode goud.	J.W.R.
October 20	Moved to ST JEAN and bivouaced in a field. Received orders to return to Château occupied on the night of Oct 19. During the day 16 Rds ammunition & S.A.A. was supplied to the 41st Bde Ammn Col.	J.W.R.
6.30 p.m. "		
October 22	Received reinforcements & completed turn-outs for 34th Brigade.	J.W.R.
October 23	Received further reinforcement of men for the Brigade.	J.W.R.
7 p.m October 24	Moved to cross roads south of St Sra in YPRES (½ mile S) Billeted in Bleaching factory.	J.W.R.

WAR DIARY or INTELLIGENCE SUMMARY

Army Form C. 2118.

(4)

October

Hour, Date, Place	Summary of Events and Information	Remarks and references to Appendices
October 26	Established Advanced Echelon of 18 Pr Amn munition column at POTIJZE.	9 pm N.B. Advanced Echelon was in its Position from dawn till dusk. J.W.H.
October 27	Moved Advanced Echelon to Pt 3 on the YPRES-HOOGE road.	
October 29	Moved to field South of T in POTIJZE. According to orders. Found French heavy battery (105 mm) in action in the field. After reconnaissance moved into Chateau at S of YPRES. Withdrew advanced Echelon.	J.W.H.
Oct. 31.	Still in same position	J.W.H.

2nd Division
XXXIV Bde R.F.A.

W A R   D I A R Y

XXXIV BRIGADE AMMUNITION COLUMN

R.   F.   A.

November

1914

Army Form C. 2118.

WAR DIARY
or
INTELLIGENCE SUMMARY.
(Erase heading not required.)

November

Hour, Date, Place	Summary of Events and Information	Remarks and references to Appendices
November 1st	Moved back to farm just above Pt of YPRES South of YPRES-MENIN road. Men billeted in barn.	J.M.H.
November 2nd	Ammunition suffered via KRUIPENDAEROE & FREZENBERG owing to shelling of YPRES-MENIN road.	J.M.H.
November 3rd	Moved to Château above Pt of POTIJZE. Men bivouaced.	J.M.H.
November 4th	Moved to farm 500× N of Point 2 on YPRES-VLAMERTINGHE road. Established advanced echelon at Château. Bivouaced.	J.M.H.
10.30 p.m. November 5th	Shells from GERMAN heavy gun falling about 300× East of bivouac; moved horses. Firing continued all night.	J.M.H.
November 6th	Moved to farm ½ a mile N of level crossing on YPRES - VLAMERTINGHE road. Bivouaced.	J.M.H.
November 10th	2nd Lieut J.V. AUSTIN left Column to join 70th Battery.	J.M.H.
November 14th	2nd Lieut T.C. CHILTON joined Column from 3rd D.A.C.	J.M.H.
November 15th	BSM. CLAYTON left Column to join the Brigade.	J.M.H.
4 p.m. " "	Received orders to move to RENINGHELST.	
7 p.m. " "	Moved to RENINGHELST. Roads bad and blocked with traffic. Billeted in the village of RENINGHELST.	J.M.H.

WAR DIARY
or
INTELLIGENCE SUMMARY.

(Erase heading not required.)

Army Form C. 2118.

(2)

November

Hour, Date, Place	Summary of Events and Information	Remarks and references to Appendices
2.15 p.m. November 19th	Moved to farm along the R. of ROUGE CROIX St. THE FLETRE – ROUGE CROIX road. 5 hundred yards God. Billeted.	J.M.H.
November 20th, 21st	Started constructing shelters for horses.	J.M.H.
November 25th	2/Lieut J.M. HOULT proceeded on leave to ENGLAND. Major F.C.L. GRIEVE proceeded on leave to ENGLAND.	J.M.H.
November 27th	2/Lieut J.M. HOULT returned.	J.M.H.
November 30th	No change	J.M.H.

2nd Division
XXXIV Bde R.F.A.

WAR DIARY

XXXIV BRIGADE AMMUNITION COLUMN

R. F. A.

3ʳᵈ–30ᵗʰ December

1914

Army Form C. 2118.

(1)

WAR DIARY
or
INTELLIGENCE SUMMARY. December

(Erase heading not required.)

Instructions regarding War Diaries and Intelligence Summaries are contained in F.S. Regs., Part II. and the Staff Manual respectively. Title pages will be prepared in manuscript.

Hour, Date, Place	Summary of Events and Information	Remarks and references to Appendices
December 3rd	Received information that Major F.C.L. GRIEVE had been granted two months sick leave.	TCC
December 14th	Major THORNTON took command of the Column.	TCC
December 16th	Captain H.B. DRESSER took command of the Column.	TCC
December 17	Major THORNTON proceeded to join 22nd Battery 34th Bde R.F.A.	TCC
	2/Lieut J.M. HOULT proceeded to join 71st Battery 36th Bde R.F.A. taking with him 2 drivers and one horse.	
	G.O.C. R.A. (Brig-Gen PERCEVAL R.A) visited the Column.	TCC
December 21st	Route marched practice of packing. Evacuated 8 horses. Sgt THOMAS promoted acting R.Q.M.S. and proceeded to 44th Bde Amm Col.	TCC
8.30 p.m. "	Received orders to be in readiness to move at 7 a.m. on Dec: 22.	TCC

WAR DIARY
INTELLIGENCE SUMMARY.
(Erase heading not required.)

Army Form C. 2118.

(2)

December

Hour, Date, Place	Summary of Events and Information	Remarks and references to Appendices
4.a.m. December 22	S.A.A. Section ordered to march at 7a.m to BETHUNE.	
7a.m.	S.A.A Section marched at 7a.m in rear of 44th Bde A.C. via STRAZEELE - MERVILLE - LOCON - BETHUNE to VENDIN. men billetted in farm ½ mile S.W. to ½ in VENDIN.	
	15 Horses with skin diseases were evacuated. Received 4 remounts 1 horse died. (Strangulation of the Bowels)	TCC
December 23.	S.A.A Section got into communication with 1st Guards Brigade & 6th Infantry Brig. cds. Suffered am- munition to former brigade.	TCC
December 24.	Rifle practice carried out.	TCC
December 25	Hard frost. Christmas presents (Princess Mary) & Christmas cards distributed.	TCC

Army Form C 2118.

(3)

WAR DIARY
or
INTELLIGENCE SUMMARY.
(Erase heading not required.)

December

Hour, Date, Place	Summary of Events and Information	Remarks and references to Appendices
December 26	Frost. Rifle practice.	
9.30 a.m.	S.A.A. Section moved under orders from O.C. B.A.C. to LE CASAN. Men billeted in farm 500 yards N of N in LE CASAN	TCC
December 27 1 a.m.	Orders to move at 7.30 a.m.	TCC
7.30 a.m.	Marched from FLETRE via STRAZEELE - VIEUX BERQUIN to PARADIS. arrived 12.45 p.m. Men were billeted.	
7 a.m.	S.A.A. Section received orders to move at 9 a.m. moved to LACOUTURE and were billeted.	
9 a.m.	SAA Section at 13th Bde A.C. in farm ½ mile W of Church in LACOUTURE.	

Army Form C. 2118.

(4)

WAR DIARY
or
INTELLIGENCE SUMMARY.
(Erase heading not required.)

December

Hour, Date, Place	Summary of Events and Information	Remarks and references to Appendices
December 28	Received 13 remounts. TCC	
December 29.	Moved to ZELOBES. Buts allotted not enough to accommodate the men. Wing garage with room to (garage) 1 mile N.W. from O.C. BAC moved to ZELOBES.	
9 a.m.	SAA Section moved to ZELOBES where it was informed billets. The 16th Section and moved to billets. TCC	
December 30th	Capt DRESSER visited billets near RICHBOURG (S' VAAST) Received 7 remounts. TCC	
December 30	2/Lt T.C. CHILTON sent on instruction. TCC	

DVL AMMN COLUMN
AUG - DEC 1914

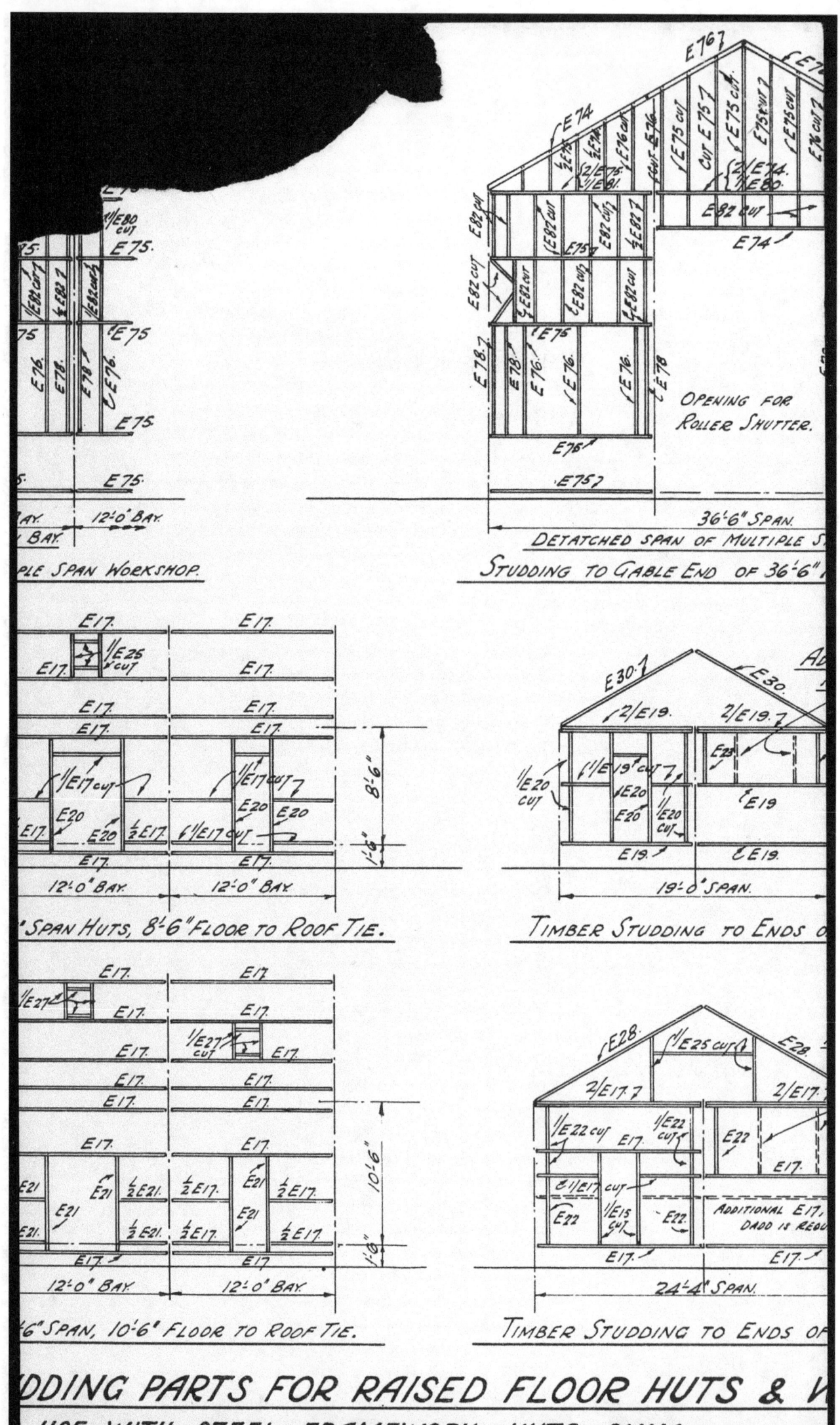

2nd Divisional Artillery.

2nd DIVISIONAL AMMUNITIOM COLUMN R.F.A.

JANUARY 1 9 1 5

2nd Div. Am. Column.

Army Form C. 2118.

WAR DIARY
or
INTELLIGENCE SUMMARY.
(Erase heading not required.)

Instructions regarding War Diaries and Intelligence Summaries are contained in F. S. Regs., Part II. and the Staff Manual respectively. Title pages will be prepared in manuscript.

Hour, Date, Place	Summary of Events and Information	Remarks and references to Appendices
1st Jany 1915 ROBECQ	Fine early - heavy rain after 4pm.	
2nd "	No. 4 billet burnt down about 5pm.	
3rd "	Fine mild day	
4th "	Showery all morning round here after 2pm	
5th "	Very wet day	
6th "	Fine morning - wet after - 2nd Lt. STUBBS & MELLOR joined from Base	
7th "	Lt.Col. W. STRONG joined from 3rd Div.	
8th "	Wet day - Capt B.L. MARRINER joined from MEERUT Div.	
9th "	Fine morning wet later. Lt. Col RAVENHILL left on posting to H.Q. Brigade.	
10th "	Very wet day.	
11th "	Fine day - rain late in evening & at night.	
12th "	Fine day.	
" "	Wet at intervals. No 4 Sect- moved billets 1 mile owing to wet ground.	
13th "	Wet morning - fine later - Major CORMES left on posting to England	
" "	No 1 Section moved billets owing to floods.	
14th "	Fine morning - Showery later.	
15th "	Fine day - 2nd Lt. STUBBS to take charge of Column wagons detached with 56" Battery att. MEERUT Div.	

Army Form C. 2118.

WAR DIARY
or
INTELLIGENCE SUMMARY.
(Erase heading not required.)

Instructions regarding War Diaries and Intelligence Summaries are contained in F. S. Regs., Part II. and the Staff Manual respectively. Title pages will be prepared in manuscript.

Hour, Date, Place		Summary of Events and Information	Remarks and references to Appendices
16th Jan 1915	ROBECQ	Fine day - mild. - Capt FARRANT posted to 34th Bde.	
17th	"	Fine day - cold & windy. - 2nd Lt O'BRIEN joined	
18th	"	Cold rost - Snow & sleet storms all day	
		2nd Lieut Barkham left on posting to 71st Battery	
19th	"	Fine milder - Horses pulls inspected by CRA 2nd Div	
20th	"	Showery - mild	
21st	"	Showery - mild	
22nd	"	Cold night - fine	
23rd	"	Fine frosty	
24th	"	Cold wind - fine	
25th	"	Cold - fine	
26th	"	Cold - fine - Section of 4.5" to 4.7 (110th Battery)	
		joined for attachment.	
27th	"	Cold - fine	
28th	"	Cold inclined to snow	
29th	"	Cold - snow showers in evening - 2nd Lt Woodward left	
		on return to England	
30th	"	Fine - warmer	
31st	"	Cold - snow storms?	

W. Strong Lt Col RFA
Comd g. 2nd Div A.C.
31-1-15

2nd Divisional Artillery.

2nd DIVISIONAL AMMUNITION COLUMN R.F.A.

FEBRUARY 1915

WAR DIARY or INTELLIGENCE SUMMARY

Army Form C. 2118.

(Erase heading not required.)

Instructions regarding War Diaries and Intelligence Summaries are contained in F. S. Regs., Part II. and the Staff Manual respectively. Title pages will be prepared in manuscript.

Hour, Date, Place	Summary of Events and Information	Remarks and references to Appendices
1st Feb ROBECQ	Fine mild – frost at night	
2nd "	Showery, fine evening	
3rd "	Fine day – 2nd Div Artillery began move to 1st Div's area	
4th " CONNEHEM	Staff & tpt – Column moved to CONNEHEM to relieve 1st Div's ammn: Col – 4.7 Section relieved MEERUT Divn	
5th "	Fine & bright – Heavy section of 1st Divn A.C. marched to other column	
6th "	Fine day – rain at night	
7th "	Fine day – rain at night – Major Symons boled to England – Only officer in Roubaix Order tonight. 25.2.15
8th "	Rain early – fine sharp	
9th "	Stormy – 7 WD wagons C.S. sent to 5th Corps with 14 H.D. horses + 7 drivers	
10th "	Frosty night – fine day	
11th "	Frosty night – fine day	
12th "	Stormy –	
13th "	Stormy	
14th "	Stormy	
15th "	Wet day	
16th "	Fine day	
17th "	Stormy, high wind & rain	
18th "	Col. R. Rundle Stewart from army, b.b.M. Isd. R.F.A. took over command. Fine –	
19th "	Wet – to be no intermedly General Koepen (4.5 how.)	
20th "	Stormy	

Army Form C. 2118.

WAR DIARY
or
INTELLIGENCE SUMMARY.
(Erase heading not required.)

Instructions regarding War Diaries and Intelligence Summaries are contained in F.S. Regs., Part II. and the Staff Manual respectively. Title pages will be prepared in manuscript.

Hour, Date, Place	Summary of Events and Information	Remarks and references to Appendices
Feb. 21 Gonnehem	Fine & bright.	
22	At fr.l. Ok inspected Column	
23. 3-4 p.m	Lt. Slatter pasted to 2/4 L. Asst. C.	
24	Party of officers and Europe below out and went to Hesdin	
25	N.C.O.s & bring him in again. Warmer later.	
26	Snowy. Wind turned out bright & Cold	
27	Fine & bright, but turned out bright & Cold	
28 LABEUVRIE RE	Cold a misty. — Instruction by Telephone to move to Labeuvrie tomorrow — moved during the morning — took over from — Off. Section I.A.C. Came with	
	Column. Maj. Hawker R.J.A. posted from III D.A.C. spare).	

B. Ramsay Fulton
Lt Col.
Comg. II D.A.C.

2nd Divisional Artillery.

2nd DIVISIONAL AMMUNITION COLUMN R.F.A.

MARCH. 1 9 1 5

WAR DIARY or INTELLIGENCE SUMMARY

Army Form C. 2118.

(Erase heading not required.)

Hour, Date, Place	Summary of Events and Information	Remarks and references to Appendices
March		
1. LABEUVIERE	Bright sunny - Cold E wind afternoon. Route I, Charges for Point I still at Lillers.	
2	Bright til day, bit cold wind. 36th Bde came to Rieulghem.	
3	Cloudy + snowy - Clouds all day.	
4	Cloudy all day.	
5	Cloudy '97 Manoeuvres for Mitrailleuse - I began 2 hours & dined A.C.C. attached for 24 hours	
6	Drill - Divines for thirty - 5 am 8th Divisional Train. 9.0 am	
7	Drill - Rained hard - Capt L. Skene posted from Sandhurst - pony holiday	
8	Col + drill - Remount Ola White	
9	Showery, high wind.	
10	Fine, cold wind. - No 11 Birth moved to vicinity Capt. Robertson (J.O) reported arrived on posting - 13 H.O horses posted -	
11	Cold, misty - 16 pa fall of snow - 8.30 pm day with transfers E. mule. 7.30 P.3 am - Broad about if don't ride up.	
12	Cold, dull - Snow bit freely here - Capt J. Simson returned from leave	
13	Cold, King Outer troop to	
14	Snow - 4 yr pp.	
15	Bright, sunny - Chas J. helo -	
16	Cold + cloudy - 8 sup, Delafontaine + trps to drill	
17	drill	
18	Fine but knows chill - No 1 Bde attacks to fire Up 7 pr Gunnedown. No 1 Bde - Lillers - D.K.C Ka. rifle when	
19	Col + drill - 4 Brig. Sim - uripro - Snow shower - 36 Bde Rd+ rangers in lillers	

Army Form C. 2118.

WAR DIARY
or
INTELLIGENCE SUMMARY.
(Erase heading not required.)

Instructions regarding War Diaries and Intelligence Summaries are contained in F. S. Regs., Part II. and the Staff Manual respectively. Title pages will be prepared in manuscript.

Hour, Date, Place	Summary of Events and Information	Remarks and references to Appendices
March Lahoussoye 20.	[illegible] — S.O. Remds — [illegible]	
21. do	Bugles all day — Remds distributed. German prisoners now in the billions	
22. do	7am = by bill — troops arrive	
23. do	4am = 2 troops transports to 113 H.R.	
24. do	7am —	
25. do	Noté ch. —	
26. do	[illegible] Relieved [illegible] — bde — 4 hrs from transport to 6 M. Acc.	
27. Longueville	all = bij 11 — seizure 14. Remds distributed, [illegible] to Longueville = [illegible]	
28. do	7am = by pck — transport 6900 — 2 bns — 4 Wagons (heavy) set from 26.4.13. Acc.	
29. do	7am = by pck —	
30. do	7am = by pck —	
31. do	7am = by/pck	

[signature]
for R.H.O.
Lt. 2/P.R.C

2nd Divisional Artillery.

2nd DIVISIONAL AMMUNITION COLUMN R.F.A.

APRIL 1915

Instructions regarding War Diaries and Intelligence Summaries are contained in F. S. Regs., Part II. and the Staff Manual respectively. Title pages will be prepared in manuscript.

WAR DIARY, II Divisional Amⁿ Column. 1

or

~~INTELLIGENCE SUMMARY.~~

(Erase heading not required.)

Army Form C. 2118.

Hour, Date, Place	Summary of Events and Information	Remarks and references to Appendices
April		
1. Fouquereuil [illegible]	Fine & bright. G.O.C. 1st Corps [illegible] came to inspect Column at 2.15 pm	
2. Do	Fine & bright. ~~[illegible]~~	
3 Do	Cloudy & damp. [illegible] all day.	
4 Do	Cloudy & dull all day.	
5 Do	Raining - Draft of 6 drivers from Havre -	
6 Do	Fine & bright - Rain afternoon - Blank day as regards Amⁿ	
7 Do	Fine & bright - Showery later - D.M.S. inspected billets -	
8 Do	Fine & bright - Showery	
9 Do	Showery, but fine latterly	
10 Do	Showery - Fine later -	
11 Do	Fine & bright - Draft 35 men from Havre	
12 Do	Fine - Draft of men distributed	
13 Do	Cloudy. But fine all day	
14 Do	Wet & cloudy - Draft of 110 horses arrd [illegible] 9.30 am - nearly all distributed by 9 pm.	
15 Do	Cloudy & [illegible] - [illegible] 2 pm.	
16 Do	Bright & fine all day -	
17 Do	Rain in night - but fine morning -	
18 Do	Bright & clear -	
19 Do	Bright & clear - Telephone established with H.Q. 2nd Divⁿ	
20 Do	Dull. [illegible]	
21 Do	Dull & drizzling - Capt. Jameson posted to 41st B.A.C. via Ravensden - Sick leave - Draft 14 men arrd for distribution.	
22 Do	Dull. Draft distributed -	
23 Do	Bright but cold [illegible] - Looked stormy later	
24 Do	Fine & bright -	

(9 29 6) W 3332—1107 100,000 10/13 H W V Forms/C. 2118/10.

Army Form C. 2118.

WAR DIARY II Division Am. Column.
or
INTELLIGENCE SUMMARY.

(Erase heading not required.)

Instructions regarding War Diaries and Intelligence Summaries are contained in F. S. Regs., Part II. and the Staff Manual respectively. Title pages will be prepared in manuscript.

Hour, Date, Place	Summary of Events and Information	Remarks and references to Appendices
April 25 Inspoernil	Review H.Q.A.G. Finished.	
26 do	Party. E units. Divi bill.	
27 do	Mostly wireless - MT Park kept one gun per B.V.I	
28 do	Zun. i. p.b.t well thing.	
29 do	Zun. strip - kept old thing.	
30 do	Full country - Wireless amately for don't know a man distributed wiphones.	

Winstanley Wilmot
Lt
Cmg. 2 Stören Am. Column

2nd Divisional Artillery.

2nd DIVISIONAL AMMUNITION COLUMN R.F.A.

M A Y 1 9 1 5

WAR DIARY
or
INTELLIGENCE SUMMARY

Army Form C. 2118.

(Erase heading not required.)

...1st Division Am? Column

Hour, Date, Place	Summary of Events and Information	Remarks and references to Appendices
May 1: FOUQUEREUIL	Bright: Draft of 1 Corp. S.S. 114 Drivers arrived from Base.	
" 2 D?	Bright - Turned cloudy + cold.	
" 3 "	Bright - mild day.	
" 4 "	Rain during night + fine evening.	
" 5 "	Rain during night + morning - Thunder storm about 3 pm.	
" 6 "	Very windy - 41st D.A.C. moved to 30th R.A.C. position. Sent Amm? orders to D.A.C.'s adopted. A good test of Am? ready - at 9 pm. acted. 10 first sent up for Div. J. 18 G? transferred to 44th (How?) Arty.	Amm. sent up between 6 am + 9 pm — 41st Bde - 6494 .18 pdr. (ind. 60 + 6E) 36 " - 60 " 44 " - 2158 4.5 How? 34 " - Nil 4.5 How?
" 8 "	Quiet: 18 G? transferred to 44th (How?) Arty. A good deal of Amm? ready - at 9 pm. orders to stand fast for Column drill during morning - heavy firing from our lines all day + many at midnight. etc. but no reply. Heavy firing from our lines all day + many guns at midnight etc.	
" 9 "	Jaire b.w. 1.05 - Very heavy firing along British Front commenced about 5 am. Still about 9 am. Got up 2005 rds. 18 pdr. in anticipation of requirements. Wire "gun" + messages from 13 h. RA Brit. Ht. 41st Bde. Sent expected + 170 rounds by Daves. Supply Party came at Zavapenne (?) Wayons Wagons rode went up in occupation - artillery. Wind W. 27 4 + 13/3 RC Area. Brilliance about 5 km. Returning empty 32 kms. about midnight. Sun Tempr. 56 Le Caian about 5 Males. Line Wind E. of foundation J. Am. moved. Inc. 31st Bde. R.A.C. returned 9 pm. etc.	Amm sent up between 6 am + 6 pm 18 Pdr 3436 - 4.5 How 520. S.A.A. 101700
" 10 "	Two little firing about 3 Sunai took our from 18 G? but 10 tons 18.4 Ht. 27 Rd. 21 etc. are obtained.	18 Pr 3260 - 4.5 - 4 2 SL 177 bdr
" 11 "	Very Little firing. Rode to La Basse in the morning.	
" 12 "	Raining slightly. Wet all day.	Amm? sent up between 8 am - 9 pm
" 13 "	Raining. Stands up in the afternoon - a great deal of thrent + sent up. Ammunition Parks.	Bde? 18 pdr - 45 6.P 544 3 1425 6 - 2 245.3 080
" 14 "	47 Div. Artillery 350. came blank for middle Divs.	34 - 6 245.3 080
" 15 "	Fine but cloudy - Two had. officers from 47 (London) Div came to arrange for temporary hospitals for 2 ambulance in Bethune. wc chilled him all day.	36 - 1646 - 240 (m-)
" 16 "	Fine. much firing in early morning. At noon heard that 1st 10 etc. had become into action. 3 times of 7 ampher - 34 M. BIll (P. Leevery + castle) - 26" D.A.C. (VERDUIGNEUL. L u? Mikes) 2 platr. Attached 7 wagons to 1st D.A.C. who have been deprived of 4th Bde. - had to supply 4 Batteries of Welsh 7. u/h? D.A.C. 2 D.A.C. Heavy Section Serving 44 R.A.C. at BETHUNE & the Advance portion of 44 D.A.C. AT LE CASAN - (5 Miles) in addition to 26 R.A.B. as usual.	26 - 144-336 60 458 - 248-1447

WAR DIARY of II Division Amn Column.

Army Form C. 2118.

INTELLIGENCE SUMMARY

(Erase heading not required.)

Instructions regarding War Diaries and Intelligence Summaries are contained in F. S. Regs., Part II. and the Staff Manual respectively. Title pages will be prepared in manuscript.

Hour, Date, Place	Summary of Events and Information	Remarks and references to Appendices
May 17 – FOUQUEREUIL	Raining. Cleared up during the morning, & good deal of firing. At 4.30 the S.C. R.A. Comr. said that the remainder of the 3rd Section was to go to join 1st D.A.C. near LOZEN, and also another complete Section. The remainder of No 3 moved off at 6 p.m. & the 2 Sect at 10 p.m. They were relieved by corresponding portions of the 1st D.A.C. at the same time. This 2 D.A.C. will now supply the 25th & 26th D.A.C. of the 1st Div. Also the 44 R.A.C. 26 Heavy Batt. as usual. Raining hard at night, when the Section arrived at 12.30 a.m.	
18 Do	Raining slightly – windy – dull all day. Heaviest demand was for 60 P. Lyddite. That came late in the evening.	
19 Do	Raining – Heard very little firing – Dull & misty all day. At Ruitton R.A.& for H.Q. moved to SAILLY-LA-BOURSE. Maj. Hawker appointed to 4? Bde. R.H.A. (8.Pck. catt⁰) from 19th	
20 CORNET MALO	Lieut. Maj. HAWKES left – appointed to 4? Bde R.H.A. Moved off at 2.30 p.m. to CORNET MALO. Leaving an 'a' Section (Henry) at FOUQUEREUIL. The I! D.A.C. Took over Billet at Festubert. At Cornet Malo found in addition say 12 2 l5? Sections that were the 35th & 40th 2 a l! Canadian H. Am.? (B⁰ P.?) attached for Amm? supply. Also Wilts Militia 5th Howr & 47? spli Hor. Brigade for Rations: slight only. Heavy firing all day. demand for Amm up to 10 p.m.	
21 Do	Fine half-misty. Heavy firing from about 9 p.m. till 15 night a early morning. W. Riding Am? D.A.C. left whilst enroute	
22 Do	Fine misty. 41! Fd taken out of Highland Brig? line & went to join the line	
23 Do	Severe Thunderstorm during the night. Ind A. trips?in the morning left FERNIE from on putting 15 & 2? D.A.C. on their full...	

WAR DIARY of II Div Am'n Column
INTELLIGENCE/SUMMARY

Army Form C. 2118.

Instructions regarding War Diaries and Intelligence Summaries are contained in F. S. Regs., Part II. and the Staff Manual respectively. Title pages will be prepared in manuscript.

(Erase heading not required.)

Hour, Date, Place	Summary of Events and Information	Remarks and references to Appendices
May 24. CORNET MALO	Fine & bright morning. A great deal of firing. N°1 Section supplied 17, 34 I.B.A.C. Proceeded to 17 DOUAI REUIS. Returned 10.30AM K.B. under Lt. 4 " DAC for Distribution. Capt. FRENCH R.H. from 16" A.C. Veterinary journal reported to H.Q. Re 2 Lorries ordered to FERFAY. Having returned the dump of 600 Hets of Pork in the morning, OTS & Ordnance on Enquiry that it would be wanted tomorrow.	18" 4.5" 6.0" SAA S THE J S S S 34 4600 228 — — — — 36 432 40 — — 6496 32,000 41 — — — — — — 35.40 — — — 100.20 — 1/Cm HP — — — — — 67,000
" 25	Fine & bright all day. The S.W. Supply Train sent for two lorries that had been lent to 35 H.A. to assist in making up their Convoy intermittent.	36 1400 240 — — — — 41 1300 260 — — 40.20 — 35.40 — — — — — — M-m HP — — — — —
" 26	Bright. Orders to march to FERFAY at 7pm. St Q " — 2nd & 3rd Section moved off at 7km & reached FERFAY at 11 pm. — were aeried on to AMIES — about 15 miles, arriving 11.40 pm. midnight. 60 (H.m.v) B att R.F.A. also billetted there. 2 lines Capt. FRENCH joined 44 " A.D. R.F.A. — 36 " Bde. R.F.A. Relieved him too.	36 1216 60 — — 30.50 — 41 800 94 — — — 45,000 1/Cm HP — — — — —
" 27 AMIES		
" 28	Dull + warm. Capt. CULLUM R.F.A. from 1 st Park posted m. adj. to Column, vice Lt. Hampton. Capt. CRAWSHAYE posted from England — joined. N°1 Section returned to Head Quarters from Longueviel having this night.	
" 29	Fine but cold. Exchanged 18 Army Gunners for Field over the 41 st Bde. & also lent them two Signallers.	
" 30	Fine & bright. 4/c R.A. + NCO visited M. Villet.	
" 31	Fine. Sept. 200 pinkles from LILLERS & sent J.B. H.D. to be entertained there. Issued 50 drivers various intelligence turns with them.	

Bradley Wilson
Lt.Col.
Com. II D.A.C.

2nd Divisional Artillery.

2nd DIVISIONAL AMMUNITION COLUMN R.F.A.

JUNE 1915

Original

WAR DIARY of 2 D.B "Ammunition Column
INTELLIGENCE SUMMARY

Army Form C. 2118.

(Erase heading not required.)

Instructions regarding War Diaries and Intelligence Summaries are contained in F. S. Regs., Part II. and the Staff Manual respectively. Title pages will be prepared in manuscript.

Hour, Date, Place	Summary of Events and Information	Remarks and references to Appendices
FOUQUEREUIL June 1st	Fine. At 5.30 am. Sec. orders to march to Fouquereuil. Capt. CULLUM. R.F.A. reported arrival yesterday. Took over adjutancy from to-day. Arrived Fouquereuil 6 pm.	
" 2	Fine & bright. Only 3.5" H. Battery and Sec. Amn. to 136,11 Battery between them Rel. (4.7") VIII Brigade.	
" 3	Cloudy + dull — 2/Lt. GRANT posted to 41st B.d.A.C. 8.9.5 Howzer 2/Lt. COFFIN posted to 2.D.A.C. in his place from 41st B.d.A.C.	
" 4	Fine all day — Artillery of Division still at rest, except 2nd D.A.C.	
" 5	Fine all day.	
" 6	Fine — 112 H.A.(M) moved in at 7pm.	
HESDINGUEL " 7	Fine — D.D.R. came & look at St. D. horses for transfer in exchange for Mules. At 10.30 pm. received orders to move to HESDINGUEL. Started off at 3.30 p.m.	
" 8	Very hot. 161 Mules + 28 drivers gained, completing the exchange of mules for H.D horses. throughout. The Column supplies for heavy Portion (8oP) of 2nd Section — A.S.C.	
" 9	Cloudy + very windy all day.	
" 10	Cloudy + damp all day.	
" 11	Cloudy, damp. Made arrangements to despatch 5'5" Surplus H.D. to the riviera. Cancelled at 7.30 pm.	
" 12	Cloudy + dull. D.D.R. came to another look at the H.D. & voted some to be returned to Mobile Section as supplies + comes L.D. Others to be distributed in the — James C. Mobile Section.	
" 13	Cargoes moved from during the day. Cloudy. A good deal of firing early + during the day. Rumounds of H.D. (40) were taken away by Dir. Farrier.	
" 14	Dull + damp morning. Capt. Crawstay orders to revert, a demand for Am. Towards the evening.	
" 15	Fine + bright. C. Demand for Am = Cheefly from 41st B.d. H.A. Capt. CRAWSTAY left to join 7th Rfz.	

Forms/C. 2118/11.

WAR DIARY of "C" Bar Ammunition Col

Army Form C. 2118.

(Erase heading not required.)

Hour, Date, Place	Summary of Events and Information	Remarks and references to Appendices
HESDIGNEUL June 16'15	Fine.	
" " 17	Fine - 55 Remounts for distribution arrived at 10 pm from Rouen - 9 to them N.A.C.	
" " 18	Fine - Portion of Remounts distributed to various units. Proportion of 18"s. & H.E. again issued.	
" " 19	Fine - 34. Rds. carried into action. Dropt 29 over for distribution - Distributed 3 pm -	
(Sunday) 20.	Fine - Distribution of Remounts continued -	
" 21	Fine but dull. Rifles & Ordce. Offr. inspected convoy 3 pm -	
" 22	Fine & hot. Very heavy firing on French left about 9.30 pm - Rained partly.	
" 23	Dull & cloudy. Clearer of later. Explosions about 2.30 pm about 3 miles S. of here.	
" 24	Dull & cloudy. Henry Portied (C.O.P?) wounded the Colonel. St. Brien had to go off after with 4 mm (Another portion) to join Reserve Division. Sgt. T. Pennett Acg.m. Rk. 2nd Cl. Sgt. Col. 2 A.S.C. accompanied by 2n Lieut. St. T. Pennett came to inspect the Column at 3 pm.	
" 25	Dull & inclined to rain - no wind. Rained most of the day.	
" 26	Fine & bright. Enemy shells caused observation balloon to descend.	
" 27 Shandy	Dull & Cloudy. Ordered 11 prs. to move our Billets - Showery evening.	
" 28	Dull & cloudy. Rec'd. Orders to be clear of HESDIG-NEUL by noon tomorrow.	
ANNEZIN 29	Dull. Marched to ANNEZIN - 3 Miles - at 11 a.m. Took over supply of 13 attaching from VIII Divn.	
" 30	Dull & cloudy. N° 1 Trench Howitzer amm'n. at 1.2.10 from 2 Bat - Fine afternoon up to 4 pm 2 Bat - Fine afternoon	

H. Endley Wilmot
Col.
Comy. 2 S.A.C.

20/15
6

2nd Divisional Artillery.
---------------- -------

2nd DIVISIONAL AMMUNITION COLUMN R.F.A.

JULY 1915

Original

WAR DIARY
of 2nd North [Midland?] Division Ammunition Column

~~INTELLIGENCE~~ SUMMARY
(Erase heading not required.)

Army Form C. 2118.

Instructions regarding War Diaries and Intelligence Summaries are contained in F. S. Regs., Part II. and the Staff Manual respectively. Title pages will be prepared in manuscript.

Hour, Date, Place		Summary of Events and Information	Remarks and references to Appendices
ANNEZIN	July 1.	Dull & cloudy - but no rain. Rd. 2/Brit. H.Q. back in Bethune.	
"	2.	Dull & cloudy - fine all day.	
"	3.	Dull. Clouds later - fell over hot.	
" Sunday	4.	Very bright - hot all day. Draft of 15 A.S.C. men arrived.	
"	5.	Cloudy & much cooler.	
"	6.	Brighter. Sent off the 15 men A.S.C. to "D" Am.S. Park H.H.Q. where they belong. 95 Remounts arrived for distribution. Major Cox attended for instruction.	
"	7.	Fine & cool. Heavy thunderstorm. Horses which held ill not to 6 pens - Remounts distributed.	
"	8.	Very windy & cool. Heavy thunderstorm from Bethune by 2/Brit. Inf. which could not be met at Park.	
"	9.	Cool & fine - Rained in the afternoon. Clouds for rest of the day.	
"	10.	Cool & fine. 2/Lt. O'BRIEN appeared & joined from Meerut Division. E.Coys.	
"	11.	Cool & windl. Received orders to move on 13th to make room for 4 Corps.	
" Sunday	12.	Dull & showery, high wind. Rec. orders to move to OBLINGHEM & moved off at 3 pm.	
OBLINGHEM	13.	Fine. Maj. Cox returned to England.	
"	14.	Fine & bright. G.O.C. R.A. came to look around in the afternoon. Rain later.	
"	15.	Fine all day.	
"	16.	Fine. 5 Wagons & 10 H.D. transferred from 48" Divn. to carry extra S.A.A. - wet afternoon.	
"	17.	Showery - 11 H.D. horses from Corentheim came & were distributed.	
" Sunday	18.	Fine.	
"	19.	Fine. S.C. R.A. came around to look for billets.	
"	20.	Fine.	
"	21.	Fine but cloudy - Am. & Parks re-organised. N° 2 Sub Park for the 2 Divisions - A draft of 2 officers & 31 U.R. arrived for distribution.	
"	22.	Fine but cloudy. 2/Lt. A.Wright posted to Column. 47 Remounts arrived for [good?] distribution.	

Army Form C. 2118.

WAR DIARY
of 2ⁿᵈ Division "Amm" Column
INTELLIGENCE/SUMMARY
(Erase heading not required.)

Instructions regarding War Diaries and Intelligence Summaries are contained in F. S. Regs, Part II. and the Staff Manual respectively. Title pages will be prepared in manuscript.

Hour, Date, Place	Summary of Events and Information	Remarks and references to Appendices
OBLINGHEM – July. 23	Fine, rather windy. Distributed Remounts	
" 24	Fine but cloudy. Showery. 6 GS. partd to 9.2 Hatty.	
" 25 Sunday	Cloudy & damp. Clewed later.	
" 26	Fine. Colonel Bradley - Wilnot went on leave. 20 O.R. arrived – 14 for First Column, Remounts for distribution. One G.S. wagon with 6 Mules received from 51st Division. 18MR for Motor Machine gun Bty. to carry	W/s N° 1 Sect — — / 2 — 3 —
" 27	Showery. Capt. Cullen returned from leave and took over command of Column during absence of Colonel. One O.R. arrived and posted to N°4 Section.	
" 28	Stormy. 9 GD² posted to 1st Brigade, 1 G.W. to 34th Bde, 4 Bre. to 36th Bde. Started to make search in every sheltering to the Column for ammunition, Rifles, Pistols etc. abandoned by troops.	
" 29	Very fine. Issued large quantities of stores etc in Village of OBLINGHEM. but sent to A.Q. R.A. 2ⁿᵈ Div¹. In all about 10 wagon loads – nearly 1 Ton of Tinned Meat at 17¾/9) Burials 5-12 pm Socks etc &	
" 30	Very fine. Two mules shot, known ? broken legs.	
" 31	Very fine. 10 O.Rs arrived for substitution.	

R.W.Cushen.

2nd Divisional Artillery.

———————

2nd DIVISIONAL AMMUNITION COLUMN R.F.A.

AUGUST 1 9 1 5

WAR DIARY of 2nd Divisional Ammn Column.
INTELLIGENCE SUMMARY
(Erase heading not required.)

Army Form C. 2118.

AUGUST 1915.

Instructions regarding War Diaries and Intelligence Summaries are contained in F. S. Regs., Part II. and the Staff Manual respectively. Title pages will be prepared in manuscript.

Hour, Date, Place	Summary of Events and Information	Remarks and references to Appendices
OBLINGHEM AUGUST 1st	Very fine. 1 Gun Posten to 34th Bde. – 5 Rnds to 36th Bde. – 4 Rnds to 41st Bde.	
2nd	Very fine.	
3rd	Showing. 1st Posten (Trains Aprivant) left for HAVRE.	
4th	Lieut Candlin, Wilmot-C. (?) back from leave.	
5th	Fine. A great many Remounts H.E. returned for repair.	
6th	Dull. The remainder of N.S. Wagon were repaired & returned to R.A.C's.	
Sunday 7th	Dull.	
8th	Dull. Enemy aeroplane very active in the evening. 37 men from Base – 16 to this Column.	
9th	Dull – windy. Party of 30 men under an officer detailed to report at Observation Station, extra 2 wagons to every station etc. 39 remounts arrived at 9 p.m. for distribution.	
10th	Very windy. Distributed Remounts – 20 Rounds for R.A. – Inspected Billets of Gordons.	
11th	Dull. Instructions to exempt Gordons on Winter Quarters cancelled.	
12th	Fine.	
13th	Dull. Shewers. 1 Section of 4th F. Section arrived up from – Capt. ROBERTSON	
14th	Fine – G.O.C. R.A. came over in the evening.	
Sunday 15th	Dull morning. Fine but inclined to be heavy. Henry Brigade about the surplus established with 2nd. –	
16th	Dull evening. Aeroplane of my 4th Section. Thunderstorm about 5 p.m.	
17th	1/ The 60th Portion of my 4th Section 2/ Henry Major R.G.A. 65 2/ Henry Transferred to 4 & 5 Section from the D.A.C. –	
18th	1/ Hd O. Boettomere & received the 104.S.A.A.4 pr portion from the D.A.C. Very wet day. Very wet. Henry shewers – changed up in the evening.	
19th	Breakfast damp. Gas Rain – Gas changed – our short Rifles for Long our not a gold for Mark VII Amm'n (about 385). 4th Amm'n Bde marched 119 Filled. Amm'n Bottomere.	
20th	Very damp – mostly but no rain all day.	
21st	Cloudy – cold – about 5.30 pm Sent off the whole of the 60 F. portion of the 4th Section to join the 2 Henry Brigade R.G.A. R.C.	

WAR DIARY of 2n Division Am. Column.

INTELLIGENCE SUMMARY

Army Form C. 2118.

Aug & Sept.

Instructions regarding War Diaries and Intelligence Summaries are contained in F.S. Regs., Part II. and the Staff Manual respectively. Title pages will be prepared in manuscript.

Hour, Date, Place	Summary of Events and Information	Remarks and references to Appendices
OBLINGHEM. Aug. Saturday. 22	Fine but cold wind.	
23	Cloudy + cold - fine later.	
24	Bright - Lt. COFFIN transferred to 9th division.	
25	Fine, but heavy ground. Went to inspect working party at BEUVRY	
26	Fine all day.	
27	Fine - Cloudy evening a little rain later.	
28	Fine - Cloudy - Rain 3 heavy about 4.30 pm	
Sunday 29	Dull - Cloudy - Rain 3 heavy about 4.30 pm	
30	Fine.	
31	Rain.	

A. Woolly Wilmot
Col.
Comg. 2 Div. A.C.
1/15 Sept.

2nd Divisional Artillery.

2nd DIVISIONAL AMMUNITION COLUMN R.F.A.

SEPTEMBER 1 9 1 5

September 1915
WAR DIARY of 2. Division Am: Column
INTELLIGENCE SUMMARY
Army Form C. 2118.

Hour, Date, Place	Summary of Events and Information	Remarks and references to Appendices
OBLINGHEM - Sept		
1.	Fine but misty. Wet evening.	
2.	Fine but misty. Revised draught. Capt. GRIFFITHS left - invalided home. Joined from Remount depot at Calais & took over command of No 1 Section 2/Lt Wright - posted to "B" Sub" R.F.A. (41? Brde).	
3.	2/Lt. WRIGHT - left on posting to 41st Bde. R.F.A. - Rainy heavy -	
3a.	Very wet all day. Commenced alloting charge in 30rv Rule Grenades, buzzer heads.	
4.	Fine. Had invitations to witness the charges in 30rv Rule Grenades, but many could not be opened, Inspected 1500 by 5pm.	
Sunday 5	Fine all day, not wet enough	
6.	Fine. Still filling Rule Grenades - about 1700 a day.	
7.	Fine but misty - still more Rule Grenades. Took over 2568 Annutts by petition from the Parks + camp + them up separately. Fine all day.	
8.	Fine - misty - All day a Jillery Rule Grenades. Sent up 2532 to 1st camp	
9.	Rain - Greater. Rule Grenades until 1 change 3120. Rain all day.	
10	Fine - misty - 1 charged Rule Grenades -	
11	Fine - misty - Still no Rule Grenades. Sent up 296 to chages, but no Petrock lighting. Saw 1st Corps about fate priority the 4th Section -	
Sunday 12	Fine - misty - Instructions came about only the 4 Section -	
13	Fine - smoky - More Rule Grenades to empty.	
14	Cloudy - warm, re - commenced on Rule Grenades. Sent up 3030. Rain and gale. Fine after 10 a.m.	
15	Full but not raining. Hd 1700rs Rule Grenades when to re-charge. Lt DUNLOP	
16	Fine but mild. Eventful.	
17	A.V.C. transferred to 34th Fd. R.A. via Lt. YOUNG A.V.C.	
17a	Fine - dull - warm. Lt. DUNLOP A.V.C. left. Lt. YOUNG A.V.C. from 34 Bde joined for duty.	

WAR DIARY / INTELLIGENCE SUMMARY

September 1915 - Cont.

Army Form C. 2118.

of 2nd Division Amm. Column

Hour, Date, Place	Summary of Events and Information	Remarks and references to Appendices
OBLINGHEM Sept. 18	Fine. Warm. Left. LE SUEUR posted to 44th Bde. R.F.A. B.A.C. on addition of 4th Section in the D.A.C. 2nd Lt. Capt. LE SUEUR left and this addition of the 4th Section completed by Employing the Hors/portion with Capt. CUSHEN to M.T.	
Sunday 19	Fine. Standard Sub. Park Troop at Flat Midt W 21.C.3 8-Ammn text 3 mins. Thus were completed between 6.30 p.m. + 9 p.m.	
20	Fine. Cool. Dull wind - Dump movement - was claimed of armn. of 75's and 13 Bde B.A.C.	
21	Fine. Cold wind. Heavy Rain 7 am N-Total of ammn. issued by D.A.C. 78 guns - 13 trophys of 4.5"	
22	Constructed 1 set arms 2 portion of ammn. thro B.A.C. (19.10/15 inclusive) arrived the armn. (18) 7/5th B.M. R.F.R. 147 hours for Distribution arranged 8.30 a.m. 30 to 5/D.A.C. 2nd Lot of 1st Bn Ammn. Colmn - Bringing walk Reph. (ory) - Report by the Remonnt distributed. 106. Rd portion of 24. D.A.C. arrived. Boer A+128 A.Y.	
23	Fine but cloudy. Heavy demand for Ammn - Thunder storm at 6.30 p.m. + 8 a.m. continued during the night	
24	Fine. Brightly. Mild - Heavy Firing. Supply Arr. + well maintained.	
25	Bright/dry - dull. 5th Army Corps g compn left. Quarry were left. 100 Rd portion of 24 B.A.C. left for BETHUNE LA B'ISAM - 75th R.P portion of Guarned 2 B.A.C. ordered to join 7th Ammn A.C. who left 5 Sept.
Sunday 26	Have been very misty. 4 Waggons during firing in the afternoon, evening.	
27	Dramp + misty - LE AIREVILLEeux Pelham joined from Remount Depot Calais 2.30 - 7 add. not a decorate. Showery afternoon. did	
28	Fine - A gale of wind + rain all night, but met much firing. Guns on the rain for next about 10.30 p.m. Sent up food to Tr 4.5" Lactory middle shite. - Heavy rain throughout - 28	1708 708 1122
29	Cloudy + damp. 138 Remounts arrived. Heavy carts moving for distribution - 75th Rd portion of Guarn 1748 422 Ammn in Reserve 2 have was told to supply 31 st Bde portion of 28 Div. 166 for the present. Went arr. with Reahb: on return y the weh. My B.C. was supplied. 29 25" 176 200 to 28 B.A.C	
30	Fine but cold. 3.8mm arrived + came for distribution	30 - 78 228 - 34

A. Pardley, Lieut Col 1/5 / 15
Army 2 D.A.C.

2nd Divisional Artillery.

2nd DIVISIONAL AMMUNITION COLUMN R.F.A.

OCTOBER 1 9 1 5

WAR DIARY
of 2nd Division Ammunition Column
INTELLIGENCE SUMMARY

(Erase heading not required.)

October 1915

Army Form C. 2118.

Instructions regarding War Diaries and Intelligence Summaries are contained in F. S. Regs., Part II. and the Staff Manual respectively. Title pages will be prepared in manuscript.

OBLINGHEM

Hour, Date, Place	Summary of Events and Information
Oct. 1.	Fine & bright – cold wind – No bom' sent up – A few shifting of troops – No.1 Column.
2.	Fine & bright – cold – Between sections bombards with heavy guns (5in.4 & 6.12"). The 7" brown horse borrowed – The 31st Bde. A.P. of Fort Chapiron of 36" Bde. Shell brought out. A party of 25 men went to dig hit ground with 6 shaps— Assisted at Portugese – relieving the 9th.
Sunday 3.	Dull – mostly – misty cold. A very large infection of Port grenades at the B.mugh. – 46.7 Bde. 1 waggon from each Bde. fetched them. Showers.
4.	Fine misty – cold – Sent 4 waggons with grenades & Bombs to 2.8" Brae. under an officer.
5.	Very dull & cold. Heavy firing during the night. No guns went to 2.8" Brae. accident – Another plan adopted – 2 Bde. sent up 4 guns of 2nd division which had been mended, also the property of the 7th division, which had dropped up as deposits of ammunition while two brigades in trenches.
6.	And changed places in the front line. Many complaints that the bomb grenades was too heavy & dropping too light – that some of the fuses were too long. By the German trench grenades. Cold, foggy – cloudy later. Sent the 34 R.B.A.C. waggons loaded up, to 6 Bde & Bde. 136, to 5.R.F. Artillery.
7.	Cold, foggy, clouds up later. – E burial D.R.C. the NCOS & Sunday opened came round to inspect billets with a view to winter Q'arters.
8.	Cold – foggy – Very heavy firing commenced about 3pm – lasted till after dark. Wind E.
9.	Cold & foggy – remained so all day. Wind N. Two 4 stretcher 4 horse ambulances from 2.8" D.A.C.
Sunday 10.	Fine – cold – Heavy firing S. from 3pm onwards.
11.	Fine – slight but heavy firing altog. about 2.30 am. R.E. commenced work on billets.
12.	Fine – foggy – thick Bay't little – 114 Harness for Australians. Very little firing.
13.	Dull - cloudy - Battle on German lines S. of Canal commenced at noon. Fine day.
14.	Cold & foggy – Some heavy firing during the day. Def. 13 men for R.A.C. militia.
15.	Very thick fog which lasted all day. Operation ceased. The troops dressed at the Windmill. Distant gunfire 3pm.
16.	Cold – foggy. R.Gen. Pearst. RAT' Corps inspected the Column at 3pm – G.R.R. 2 Bd. + Staff Capt. come with him – A good deal of grumbling of Brig. still going on.
17.	Cold – foggy – brighter later. 7" Division went out – 2.8" Bde. part of 1st Corps.
18.	Cold & foggy – A.P. billets.
19.	Cold – foggy – Very heavy firing about 5.7pm. Orders came at 8pm to exchange 200 L.D. Fur 200 H.D. horses from with the 2.D.S.T. divis. Bris day.
20.	Very cold – damp. Sent off 200 L.D. horses in exchange for 160 H.D. & H. 2.8" Division.

October 1915 - 2nd Sheet. Army Form C. 2118.

WAR DIARY
of 2nd Division Ammunition Column

INTELLIGENCE SUMMARY
(Erase heading not required.)

Instructions regarding War Diaries and Intelligence Summaries are contained in F. S. Regs., Part II. and the Staff Manual respectively. Title pages will be prepared in manuscript.

Hour, Date, Place	Summary of Events and Information	Remarks and references to Appendices
OBLINGHEM. Oct.		
21	Cold + foggy. Rained hard at 9 pm. 182 D. did not go as a Regt from 28 Brigade arrived.	
22	Cold + foggy.	
23	Very wet + foggy.	
24 Sunday	Very wet. Foggy. Heavy rain. 2.30 pm. Capt. Lewis orders to Eth. Command of 4 1st B.A.C.	
25	Raining hard. 4 Sergeants ordered home on promotion to New Armies. Capt Lewis left 6 Ten Commd J 36 B.A.C. - very wet all day. Fine but cold wind - 18? L.D. Remounts arrived from depôt, remainder of	
26	H.D. horse from 28 BDE returned to Remounts.	
27	Raining - but cleared later - no sun.	
28	Wet. Cloudy. rained all day.	
29	Cloudy - damp, but no sun.	
30	Cloudy, a damp but warmer.	
31 Sunday	Fine - cold - windy - but not much rain - heavy firing in the afternoon down Vermelles direction.	

Woodley Wilmot
Lt.
Cmdg. 2 Divl.

1/15
Ld

2nd Divisional Artillery.

2nd DIVISIONAL AMMUNITION COLUMN R.F.A.

NOVEMBER 1915

WAR DIARY
of the 2nd Division Amm. Column
INTELLIGENCE SUMMARY

(Erase heading not required.)

Nov. 1915 - Sheet 1

Army Form C. 2118.

Hour, Date, Place	Summary of Events and Information	Remarks and references to Appendices
OBLINGHEM - Nov.		
1	Raining + continued all day.	
2	Raining early, shift winds.	
3	Gave two weeks Major Carden returned from leave and took over command.	
4	do.	
5	do.	
6	do.	
7	do.	
8	do.	
9	do.	
10	Gun. Serious accident in No 3 Section Lines caused by explosion of two 18pr. H.E. Shells at 2.30 p.m. 10111 Bdr Horsley H. and 67970 St Hackman G.W. Killed. Sgt Lavey P.B. 32369, Cpl Jube T.29945, Bdr French W. 29626, Bdr Porter J. 14508, Bt Courtney A.S. 10330 G, St Slagg J. 9790 7, Bt Bonfield W. 77986, and Br Palmer W. 27881 wounded. One Mule mortally wounded and one slightly wounded, 48 Mules exchanged for 48 H.D. horses, all complete with harness, at HAVERSKERQUE with MEERUT DIVISION.	
11	Gun. Cont. of Burying. Field on the above accident.	
12	do. 6th Ex 34 of enlistment returned	
13	Raining - whole unit. Cleaned lakes. Lieut. M.F. COURAGE from No 2 Sect. vice Capt. FERNIE. Capt. EARDLEY-WILMOT returned from [illegible] - to command [illegible] - returned. Lieut. DRAKE from Indian Corps posted temporarily	posted to
14	Gun. wet - Lieut. Wightwick to take over duty of Adjutant.	
15	Frosty and cold day has told us went to same trotter. South Lieut. WESTON joined from 16th Bd. R.F.A. L. PELHAM posted to 36 B.A.C.	
16	Frosty. Rec: information that Area had been allotted to HQ Me Coleman wanted proceed to ZOUQUIRES les BETHUNE.	
17	Cold, damp. rained during the day. Two mea & country cart from Thorvane to Windles - Repn on for the 33rd Division.	

November 1915 - 2nd Sheet.

WAR DIARY
of 2nd Division Am[munition] Column
INTELLIGENCE SUMMARY
(Erase heading not required.)

Army Form C. 2118.

Hour, Date, Place	Summary of Events and Information	Remarks and references to Appendices

OBLINGHEM - Nov.

18. Hoar frost. Capt. CULLUM left to join the 9th B[de] RFA - 36th Bde. Lieut. DRAKE took over the duties of Adjutant. Capt. Winckler C of E "detached" from H.Q. R.A.

19. Frosty. Ordinary dumps.

20. Cold. Change. Transferred 21 H.D. to Bri. Train. Ammunition (Rounds)

21. Cold. Manage. Salt same H.D. horses away to mobile Veterinary Corps. Veterinary — Col. 36 L.P. with harness from Indian Corps for distribution.

Sunday

22. Frosty & cloudy. Bought 65 drivers from Base for distribution.

24. Hoar frost. Arrived in the evening —

25th. Frosty, cloudy - A little rain in the evening.

26. Frosty & Sunny - Rain at night.

26. Wind & showery - 2/Lt. ... 1.S.S. joined from base. Left party of 4 D Bde. 22 Gunners, 2 S joined from Depôt. Two Sgt hospitalised under sentence.

Gave out some educational ... about 50 tons of

27. Proceed to FORD QUIERES by BETHUNE - Having being short of harness & deficient 4 ans in Boards & Greatcoats being short of harness & deficient of 100 horses, we had to have 2 lorries to move the Am: & then did not finish the one - Frosty — Lieut. SABINE struck off strength.

28. Hoar frost — Bombardment in progress. Bivouac

29. Hoar frost. Turned train about 10 acres & removed all dung. A great deal of dust Nov. to hand up.

FOUQUIERES

30. November. dumps 2/Lt. T.J.C. MOOLMAN and 2/Lt. H.T. WOODFORD were posted to the Column. ... approximately 24 horses & 24 Mules without harness were brought from late Indian Corps Div. Train.

1/15
1/12

A. Smalley - W[ing?]l Col
Comm[ande]g 2 D.A.C.

2nd Divisional Artillery.

2nd DIVISIONAL AMMUNITION COLUMN R.F.A.

DECEMBER 1915

Sheet 1

Dec. 1915

WAR DIARY of 2nd Division Ammunition Column
INTELLIGENCE SUMMARY
(Erase heading not required.)

Army Form C. 2118.

Instructions regarding War Diaries and Intelligence Summaries are contained in F. S. Regs., Part II. and the Staff Manual respectively. Title pages will be prepared in manuscript.

Hour, Date, Place	Summary of Events and Information	Remarks and references to Appendices
FOUQUEREUIL - December 1	Raining - Clement Later - Capt. LANIGAN R.F.A. Rejoined from his course. Posted to troop A - Capt. OSBORN - 2/Lt WEIMAN R.F.A. & A. Kreft 4	
	2.5 men joined.	
	2 Fine. L. Bradley Went attached temporarily to 41st R.F.A.	
	Major W. Winter assumed command of 2nd D.A.C.	
3	Raining	
	Sends Webber & Mellor on leave to England. Raining & blowing hard.	
4	No 58453 Dr Halliday H No3 Sec died suddenly at about 5.30 P.M.	
Sunday 5	Raining and high wind	
6	Raining and high wind	
7	Drivr Murpain No 3 Sec attached to 44 R.A. 6 temporarily.	
	1 S.S. + 5 Drivers posted to 31st Bde R.F.A. 6 gnrs + 4 Drs posted to 36th Bde R.F.A.	
	11 gnrs + 11 Drs posted to 4th Field R.F.A.	
8	Reexchanged 4/14 L.D. with the 46 Div Amm Col for 2/78 H.D.	
	Wagons returned from the Bois de Riette.	
9	83 N.C.O.s + men posted to 2nd Siege from Reserve.	
10	Raining	
11	Fine. L.	
Sunday 12	Fine. Col. Bradley - Wilmott returned to Column.	
13	Line WI	
14	Fine 1.83 Remounts arrived for distribution	
15	From Corbet - Distributed Remounts. Capt S. W. GRIFFITH posted to 44 K.D.A.C.	
16	Drizzling - But fine + warm later	
17	to be + damp. Raining a great deal.	
18	Dull, damp. At 1.30 p.m. G.O.C. Division with Staff & G.O.C. R.A. LDiv. with L.O.H. Capt. Connor sees the Column & Horses the Accomodation of Horses & Personnel.	

Sheet 2. Dec. 1915

WAR DIARY of 2. Division Am. Column

INTELLIGENCE SUMMARY

Army Form C. 2118.

Instructions regarding War Diaries and Intelligence Summaries are contained in F. S. Regs., Part II. and the Staff Manual respectively. Title pages will be prepared in manuscript.

(Erase heading not required.)

Hour, Date, Place		Summary of Events and Information	Remarks and references to Appendices
FOUQUERES-	Dec. 19	Fine & bright.	
	20	Front Col. Hall. D.D.R. & D.D.V.S. came. 4 O.H.D. Frangipani to 47" Div.	
	21	Raining - not all day.	
	22	Cold & damp. Lieut WESTMANpost to 71"Bde? Lieut. THOMAS posted to D.A.C.	
	23	Raining slightly. Remount.	
	24	Wet & muddy.	
	25	Cloudy & dull - Capt. COURAGE posted Captain.	
Sunday	26	Fine. Three officers from 33 Div attached for Instruction.	
	27	Cloudy & wet	
	28	Fine all day & warm.	
	29	Cold & foggy - Sent a party of 20 B supp ors under Lt. Boyd to Etrun return 31/12/15	
		602.T.T.Chu. about 4 OMCCH2amm. Fine all day.	
	30	Fine. Officers & 3 officers returned to their Brigades. 3 others came. Capt Y	
		17 grooms & Batmen from R.a.C.	
	31	Fine -	

A. Eadley Wilmot
Col.
Comdg. 2 D.A.C.

2ND DIVISION
DIVL ARTILLERY

2ND DIVL. AMMN COLUMN R.F.A.

JAN - DEC 1916

2nd Divisional Artillery.

2nd DIVISIONAL AMMUNITION COLUMN R.F.A.

JANUARY 1916.

WAR DIARY of 2nd Division Am'n Column
INTELLIGENCE SUMMARY

Army Form C. 2118.

(Erase heading not required.)

January 1916. 1st Sheet.

Instructions regarding War Diaries and Intelligence Summaries are contained in F. S. Regs., Part II. and the Staff Manual respectively. Title pages will be prepared in manuscript.

Hour, Date, Place		Summary of Events and Information	Remarks and references to Appendices
FOUQUIERES - Jan.	1	Wet & cloudy.	
Sunday	2	Fine but dull. Heavy demand for Am'n in the evening.	
	3	Stormy + dull. Fine at times all day. Staff officers from 3rd Bd. left.	
	4	Fine. Furious dull and cold. Col. Bartley Wilmot R.A. att'd to take command	
	5	O.R.A. II Div. Major Bucker RFA. assumed command.	
		Fine. Captain Osborne R.A.M.C. returned from leave is employed	
	6	Dull and windy. Lieut. Wootten R.A.M.C. left to join 17 Fusiliers (Reserve Batt) pending	
	7	still a homely 3rd Lieut. Hartman posted to 15 Bdey, 2nd Bd. Park.	
	8	Fine. 53 amounts received	
Sunday	9	Fine. Col. Bartley Wilmot returned from H.Q. R.A.	
	10	Fine. Lt. Morgt + party returned from Berick Vieppe.	
	11	Rain all day.	
	12	Fine still. 6 f'on other. It rained - 65 Remount issued for distribution.	
	13	Cloudy - windy but warm. Dropt of 13 men issued transferred & transs.	
	14	Fine.	
	15	Fine. Move in exchange with 12. D.A.C. cancelled.	
Sunday	16	Fine. Capt. Courage posted to 44 R.A.C. vice Griffith.	
	17	Fine. Capt. Courage joined 44 R.A.C.	
	18	Dull but no rain.	
	19	Fine - 2 Div. R.A. taking over from 12 Div. R.A. N.9 Camel. but the	
		O.R.C.'s and amgt amt.	
	20	Fine - dull -	
	21	Fine - dull.	
	22	Fine - Rained in the afternoon -	
Sunday	23	Fine - inclined to frost - Sent 24 men to Battain.	
	24	Fine - dull.	
	25	Fine - bright.	
	26	Fine - dull -	
	27	Fine - dull -	
	28	Fine - dull. Col. d. Rudyf Rifles 35a. took over command. Col. Bartley Wilmot	
	29	Fine - dull. Col. Bartly Wilmot proceeded to England.	
	30		

2nd Divisional Artillery.

2ND DIVISIONAL AMMUNITION COLUMN R.F.A.

FEBRUARY 1916.

WAR DIARY
OF
INTELLIGENCE SUMMARY
(Erase heading not required.)

February 1916 Vol. 2

Army Form C. 2118.

Instructions regarding War Diaries and Intelligence Summaries are contained in F.S. Regs., Part II. and the Staff Manual respectively. Title pages will be prepared in manuscript.

Hour, Date, Place	Summary of Events and Information	Remarks and references to Appendices
FOUQUIERES. Feb 1.	Fine. colder. Capt. Finlay 3" D.G. joined to command No 2. Section.	
" 2"	Fine - cold. 22 men joined from Base details.	
" 3"	" - had S.E. with Genl Stokes re Corp Div came round.	
" 4"	" - Hanmer. Thurkard evening. Some rain.	
" 5"	Some rain - Sir wm. Pulteney at night. Very fine all day. Capt Belleville	
" 6"	Coy joined at night to Command No 3 Section.	
" 7"	Fine & wet. colder -	
" 8"	Lt Col Johnstone 33rd D.A.C. came - to stay for instruction. gave Ra 2nd Div came round here	
" 9"	D.D.R. O'Brien came to change to L.D. I.O.9. infantry carriages.	
" 10"	11.50 O'Brien on leave. W. Thomas 9ath.	
" 11"	Conference at Div Artty re "Beauport". Col. Johnstone attended. Lt Col Johnstone left. 6 men of 33rd D.A.C. came for instruction. Sir J.	
" 12"	Home Campbell came as adjt. -	
" 13"	S.E. + E. Gale. much colder - Rain & cold -	
" 14"	No church - moved men of H.Q. down to coal hrus -	
" 15"	Heavy fall all day. Cleared streight S.W. wind	
" 16"	Div? moving out t front: sent 4 H.D. horse to 7. RHA. - got 8. L.D. remounts, 4 to 68 to 23, thus 59 details joined as reinforcements. Heavy S.W. gale all day. Some shelter from stores, Div pay out & rest. began repl April 119.120 trades (38.28 Drive). -	Supplied by Sign by Lt Col R.H.A. COMDG 2ND D.A.C. 2 hours

WAR DIARY

INTELLIGENCE SUMMARY

(Erase heading not required.)

Army Form C. 2118.

Vol. 2

1916.

Hour, Date, Place	Summary of Events and Information	Remarks and references to Appendices
FOUQUIERES Feb 1917	Fines. New wind. 6 men joined from Base Details.	
19	48 hour draftee to Base – 20 others from No1 MO in charge of S/Lt LD. 10.10 am No2 draftee 6. Major d W Lauder assumed Command of Column from Base. 3 pm No1, 3 from No2 drafted to Div Train, 44 LD 74 in the same	
20	10.10 am Sub Section 41st B.A.C. attached.	
21	Fine. Sub Section 41st B.A.C. left Column. Lieut Sir J Home Campbell to Divisional in Base.	
22	Fine.	
23	Snow. 9 L.D. arrived from Base.	
24	Snow.	
25	Slight thaw. Received supply of ammunition.	
26	Snow & frost.	
27	Snow & slight thaw.	
28	Fine but still. Case of infection disease reported at Bétourné Lorraine. Bétourné immediately cleared of troops and put out of bounds.	
29	Column moved to BARLIN during the day.	

2nd Divisional Artillery.

2nd DIVISIONAL AMMUNITION COLUMN R.F.A.

MARCH 1916.

Army Form C. 2118.

WAR DIARY
or
INTELLIGENCE SUMMARY
(Erase heading not required.)

Vol III
1916.

Instructions regarding War Diaries and Intelligence Summaries are contained in F. S. Regs., Part II. and the Staff Manual respectively. Title pages will be prepared in manuscript.

Hour, Date, Place	Summary of Events and Information	Remarks and references to Appendices
BARLIN. March 1st	2/Col. Chas. Platt Saylor returned from leave, having been to FOUQUIERES	
2nd	On 29th ult. Col. left — sunset — Fair trek — arranging billet at LAUTEY CITE. but move cancelled after arrangements made —	
3rd	Very wet — 1 Sec. 47th DAC coming — to be attached.	
4th	Heavy rainstorm in rfk. 75 Remounts (horses). A.D.V.S. & D.V.S. arr. at see about manage stable being inspected. It is now of the description	
5th	Zinc disputed clothing at church parade. Generally in a bad state. Supt. 9.23 B.M. camp all out of H.D. but 4 myself sent away & horse.	
6th	G.D. snow. Sent 60 men to B.A.C.s billed at 3rd arty	
7th	v. cold. remained all day.	
8th	Slipped at myself fell for morning. Arranges Khaki over & temp. ind. took H.Ok. of trench army. etc. 1st, 2nd Section —	
9th	G.D. snow. have trouble getting winter never killed.	
10th	wet & dull — 18 mules came fr. Column, amongst 89 for this unit. 6.10 p.m. Funeral section.	
11th	wet & dull - Mess & S.U. in Barlin.	
12th	Finale — routine —	
14th		
15th	— Sec. 47th D.A.C. left 8.23 a.m. C. (sec) came in to line —	
16	— Routine —	

WAR DIARY or INTELLIGENCE SUMMARY

Army Form C. 2118.

Vol III 1916

Hour, Date, Place	Summary of Events and Information	Remarks and references to Appendices
BARLIN Mar. 17th	Dull & overcast – mild. Routine. Stablemen & scrapmen work on cranes.	
18th	Fine – routine –	
19th	Fine – Church parade – clothing better but turn out requires more attention. 1 N.C.O. + 20 men for guard fatigue in trenches –	
20th	Fine & rain.	
21st	Dull & rain.	
22nd	Very wet. Dull & cold. Draft of 39 men from home.	
23rd	Dull cold – arranging billets at BRUAY. Draft 4 men from home – fatigues etc. –	
24th	Deep mud & snowed all morning. Marched by sections to BRUAY – leaving 237 D.A.C. last seen in by 12.30. Billets had a very scattered. 165 mules, horses for DAC came at night & got them up by 9-30 p.m. – packed & spent a bad night. Finding a D.A.C. D. Remount work is bad policy, since cannot be satisfactory & wastes by very arms. Must be large –	
BRUAY 25th	Stormy, wet & snow. Half the column wagon lines parked soft whole scale of arms – the others empty. In fatigues & overhauling. Third stone by Remounts – 10's to D.A.C. –	
26th	Wet & stormy – cold. Sent 21 A.m. 1 G. Sgr to Batteries – when were remount details.	
27th	Wet & stormy – routine – changed some billets – usual remount details –	
28th	Hard gale (scarcely AW). Sent 4 wagons, drivers + horses complete to 47th Bde. In alteration of establishment.	

Army Form C. 2118.

WAR DIARY
or
INTELLIGENCE SUMMARY

Vol III

1916.

(Erase heading not required.)

Hour, Date, Place	Summary of Events and Information	Remarks and references to Appendices
BRAY March 29"	Played F.S. in rifle . read.	
30"	Fine. Draft of 21 O.R. came from home. D.B.E came round in afta	
31st	Fine. Routine	S/Fowler.Hy.Offr. +C.L. Comdg 2nd Bn ACol

2nd Divisional Artillery.

2nd DIVISIONAL AMMUNITION COLUMN R.F.A.

APRIL 1916.

WAR DIARY
or
INTELLIGENCE SUMMARY

(Erase heading not required.)

Vol IV
1916

Army Form C. 2118.

Hour, Date, Place	Summary of Events and Information	Remarks and references to Appendices
BRUAY April 1st	Fine – B.O.C. R.A. inspected Col in lines. However gunners were attentive yet also reported Band quartet among personal friendly after one welcome tournament. Fatigues & routine	
2nd	Fine Gun Drill – routine	
3rd	Fine Lectures & routine	
5th	Fine 9.00 2 Divn inspected B.A.C. in marching order on road. Satisfactory	
6th	Fine – cold. Brig Gen Geddes C.R.A. 4th Corps came round lines. Lieut Thomas and Lootford returned from Sch of Arty. 2/Lt Lootford in arrest for Gard. Maj Austen cont on leave	
7th	Fine cold – Draft 14 gnrs – 6 gnr joined from base – partly replenished. Weather was teeming	
8th	Fine cold. 2/Lt Wilkins posted to 34th Rifle 5.0" Batty	
9th	Fine Church parade in tour.	
12th	Very wet & windy. Draft of 27 men from Base came. All have stopped	
13th	Gales + rain – Men from bomb school returned & went on to Dieval.	
15th	Gales, snow & rain continue. 2/Lt O'Brien posted to 114th Rifle	
16th	rain – cold wind. 1 man sent to hospital from Base, gnr not arrived.	
17th	Rain & Gale. Maj Austen returned from leave.	Reports Capt Melville inefficient
18th	Do. Do. Genl C.M. on Lt Lootford – adjourned.	and added to his unsuitable
19th	Do. Do. 28 troopers on fatigue to report at BARLIN tomorrow. 114 temperament also	movably.
	Remounts for Divn came (5th DAC). 20 reinforcements also 3 left on railway en route.	

WAR DIARY or INTELLIGENCE SUMMARY

(Erase heading not required.)

Army Form C. 2118.

VOL V
1916

Hour, Date, Place	Summary of Events and Information	Remarks and references to Appendices
BARLIN. April 20th	Fair to showery. Moved back to BARLIN during morning. A subsection of 23rd R.A.M.C. being left to Concentration road. Billet & lines v. dirty.	
21st	Fine (cold) wind - routine. Many fatigues.	
22nd	Very wet all day. Insp. Graham went to hospital. 2nd C.M.R. shoot pd.	
23rd	Fine & clear. Inspns run hung & wrote protests as all men are being up as work casuals from R.H.Q, M.G. & St Cpls R.A. Gun out to Quiercust [?]. Sent 13 gn & 12 gn to Matheres, 2 gn & 3 mules slightly wounded at HERSIN on fatigues. Lt Weston to hospital.	
24th	Fine. Insp. Hart came for a day's instruction.	
25th	Fine. Routine.	
26th	Fine. R.t. A draft of 13 gn & 11 gn came from home. Reported to Lt Lount[?] for extra para 10th K.R.	
27th	Fine - R.t.	
28th	Fine & R.t. 9.0.C R.A. G.H.Q. came in afternoon. Lt Golding joined from home.	
29th	Fine - R.t.	
30th	Fine R.t. Lt Golding to 24 Brig.d. Draft of 20 gn 13 gn went to Matheres. Temp/Lt Lodery joined from home.	

S/Zyxxhalix May Lt Col
Co. 9/2 DAC

2nd Divisional Artillery.

2nd DIVISIONAL AMMUNITION COLUMN R.F.A.

M A Y 1916.

WAR DIARY or INTELLIGENCE SUMMARY

Army Form C. 2118.

Vol VI 1916

2 Div Am Col

Instructions regarding War Diaries and Intelligence Summaries are contained in F.S. Regs., Part II. and the Staff Manual respectively. Title pages will be prepared in manuscript.

Hour, Date, Place	Summary of Events and Information	Remarks and references to Appendices
BARLIN May 1st	Routine - fine -	
2nd	Fine & breezy. To Div H.Q. at Hersford.	
3rd	Routine. Cooler. Draft of 9 Drivers from Base.	
4th	Fine. Wind in E. Very hot in evening.	
5th	V. hot & squally. Sent 92 L.D. horses to Bethune. 201 Remounts for Div. came at night. - 108 mules to B.A.C.	
6th	Fair. Distributed Remounts to units. -	
7th	Wet - cooler - Routine & Church.	
8th	Fine, cold wind. Maj Craken returned from hospital.	
9th	Wet & stormy.	
10th	Dull to fair. Draft of 40 gnrs & 20 Drs came from Base.	
11th	- Routine -	
12th		
13th	Very wet & dull.	
14th	Fair - cold - Sent draft of 31 gnrs & 26 Drs to Brigades -	
BRUAY 15th	Wet & fine. H.Q. & 2nd & 3rd Secs moved to BRUAY in morning (1st Sec remaining in to serve Brigades still in..)	
16th	Dull & fine - yesterday Reported supplies & difficulties for the purposed reorganisation of Am. Cols - "Offg & Smith (Dir) Repts to A.D.V.S., came round on inspect, Q.O.C. R.Q. 1st Army came on visit. G.O.C. R.Q. 1st Army came and inspected stables in aftn. Temp. to lordship above	
17th	Fine A.D.V.S, came round on inspect. horse & fine H.O.	

WAR DIARY or INTELLIGENCE SUMMARY

Army Form C. 2118.

Vol VI 1916

Hour, Date, Place	Summary of Events and Information	Remarks and references to Appendices
BRUAY May 18th 1916	Lt. Col. Hu Mul Taylor DSO R.F.A. proceeded on leave to England. Major G. Buchan assumed command of 2nd D.A.C.	
19th	Fine. 2/Lieut Woodford R.F.A. returned to England to report to W.O.	
20th	No 1 Sec lost 7 G.S. wagons rejoining Column from BARLIN.	
21st	Fine	
CAUCOURT 22nd	Column less 7 G.S. wagons moved to CAUCOURT. Fine	
GAUCHIN LEGAL 23rd	Column less 7 G.S. wagons moved to GAUCHIN LEGAL. 3600 rounds of 18pr issued. Fine	
24th	Issued 3600 rounds 18pr and 12.16 (4.5 How) Fine	
25th	Rain.	Captain Gourage R.F.A. retired Scale R.F.A.
26th	Took over details of 44 Bde (37 W.O. N.C.O.'s & other ranks) (L.D. 40) (Vehicles 7) Reorganized 2nd D.A.C. to new organization. Formed new T.M. Battery consisting of 6 6 other ranks (V 2 Heavy T.M. designation) 3 G.S. wagons to Bde.	Reinforcements sent to Bdes. 14 opr 9 dvr. T. Potier 29 L.D. 1 H.D. 3 officers joined (M. Maxwell B. Chandrill) No.4
CAUCOURT 27th	Sent to Base as surplus to new establishment. 1 officer, Captain Bellville R.F.A. 136 (N.C.O's+men) Horses 118 Mules 142 G.S. Wagons 38 S.A.A. Carts 3 Telephone Cart 1 Bicycles 5 Harness 1411 Sets Saddlery 6 Sets Rifles 248 Artificers Cart 5 Bres. Lieut Thomas R.F.A went with this party to assist.	

	Not Establishment	Est. New Head	Officers	Other Ranks	Z.D. + Riders	Horses	Mules	Vehicles	18 Pr	4.5 How	G.S. Limbers	G.S. Cart	W.D. Cart	Water Carts
	173			748	191	358	224		18	4	4	4	1	
		202	18						12	4	4	8	1	
									4			12		

28th	3 B.A.C's joined 2 D.A.C. to form new sections. H.Q. 2 D.A.C. moved to CAUCOURT 4th Section moved to HERIPRE. The B.A.C.'s joining up at CAUCOURT. Fine. 20 O.R. sent up to 3 b Bde H.Q. trench digging. 20 G.S. wagons sent to No1 Sec by 4 sec to take up 4.5 How Amn. Adjutant went forward at 7 p.m.	
29th	Fine. 20 teams (4 horses) were sent to 2nd DA. Train. C.O. returned at 7 p.m.	
30th	Very heavy rain in night & followed all very wet. 7 wagons of 4 sec returned from BARLIN.	
31st	Fine A 235" th came in to Column close by, at GAUCHIN - LEGAL	

S/ Arthur L.O. Poy Lt Col
COMDG. 2ND. D.A.C.

2nd Divisional Artillery.

2nd DIVISIONAL AMMUNITION COLUMN R.F.A. ::

JUNE 1916.

WAR DIARY or INTELLIGENCE SUMMARY

Army Form C. 2118.

2 D Am Col
Vol 23

VOL VI
1916.

Hour, Date, Place	Summary of Events and Information	Remarks and references to Appendices
CAUCOURT June 1st	Fine – all papers shipped for afternoon. Ambulance alright.	
2nd	Fine – G.O.C. Ra rode round Sections. D.296 left am to lie up — Bn. Adj. H.Q. moving.	
3rd	Fine – cold wind. A fire at a farm at HERIPRE. at 6 pm. No. 4 Sec. (a) Men & Canteen there, but none killed in buildings. Some harness etc destroyed.	
4th	Dull – cold wind.	
5th	Fair windy. Routine. Hours of work little on 31st. This new organisation does not seem to give much scope to a M.T. gnr. a G.O. Too many controls in arrangements of ammn. supply, my bad experience A. Echelon works better. Quiet [illegible] supplies + Staff Offr. must have control of Ammn. Transport. An accident to Gun mouth. have no particular platform except a appears there no indian Coys. — mobile reserve under Corps.	
6th	Windy & stormy. Heavy rain storms. hy. Oakam suit —	
7th	Fair + fine. Heard of Lord Kitchener lost in H.M.S. Hampshire.	
8th	Dull + mild. Routine.	
9th	Fair to fine. Sir J. Horne Campbell K.C.B., struck off strength 2nd Canad Div'l Am. Col — posted to No. 2. L.C.C.	
10th	Fair to fine. Heavy thunderstorm. New draw in & now state V.2. +.M. Mallory arrived from Gunnery School + Mjr Ruiz & Fulls.	

WAR DIARY or INTELLIGENCE SUMMARY

Army Form C. 2118.
Vol VII
1916

Hour, Date, Place	Summary of Events and Information	Remarks and references to Appendices
June — CAUCOURT	11ᵗʰ Wet & stormy. Heavy thunderstorm —	
	12ᵗʰ Hot, cold + dull. V.2 T.M. battery left. —	
	13ᵗʰ Hot+cold — line busier every hr. State. 2 O'Brien posted as appt. mi Water.	
	14ᵗʰ Weather improving — found draping. Arrangements to dump + L'O'Brien took over duties of Asst DWester opened his section.	
	15ᵗʰ Still + milder. 1ˢᵗ consignment of Dump amm sent up to Refill Pt (amm) protested again on finer wire for the plan altered. Arranged new Dump at GAUCHIN LEGAL. — 25 O.R. reinforcements came from base.	
	16ᵗʰ Mild to fine. 47ᵗʰ Bde A.C. (see) Lyt. detachment of 2 Sec. 47ᵗʰ D.A.C. came in the attached). Schult J. 4. Crosby Stƒ Q. came in. began proper Dump + R.P at GAUCHIN LEGAL	
	17ᵗʰ Fine — cold N.E. wind. Army at rest. Dump + R.P.	
	18ᵗʰ Fine cold — Dump filled up & ready for use. Filled up 'B'. Echelon of T/223. — sent 159 mules. 2 offrs + 128 men to TILLERS-au-BOIS to take over French Railway —	
	19 Dull - cold. Moved GAUCHIN Dump up to CAUCOURT — a good day's work, beginning at 6 am. under Capt Ferrie. Horse hort 14,000. A + 1000 B in stock. —	
	20ᵗʰ Rain. Draft of 12 NCOs + men joined fr. base —	
	21ᵗʰ Fine warm.	

WAR DIARY
or
INTELLIGENCE SUMMARY

Vol VII
1916

Army Form C. 2118

Hour, Date, Place	Summary of Events and Information	Remarks and references to Appendices
CAUCOURT.		Linen A⋆ B⋆
22ⁿᵈ	Fine warm. 80 Remounts for Div. came at night. 6 S.D. for Div. Col.	— 76 264
23ʳᵈ	D.D.R. + Army came round. Took 2 M.D. Fine – hot. Thunderstorm in evening. 4 compy schedules from 223ʳᵈ Army Am. Col. Sqdn.	684 760
24ᵗʰ	Mild – heavy showers. 2/Lt Grover to D/36 Mth Bty —	608 1672
25ᵗʰ	Fine warm. 2/Lt Kingston posted from D/36 Mth Bty —	— —
26ᵗʰ	Fine – very heavy showers all day. – B.Q.M.S. Sexton — Joined 4ᵗʰ	
27ᵗʰ	Hot – heavy showers –	
28ᵗʰ	Hot + dull. Staffing so good from Bruce. Arranged with Staff Capt. after a tactical walk for new Organization. Moved No 1 Section on to the hill on their Guns and reprovy 1977 of remnts	
29ᵗʰ	warm. Smiths Coy of 9 facts. Brute is calling attention of newly 9 mmts deserters back to H.Q. and a Echelon in lieu of 14 fr H.Q. + 1 section for each section —	
30ᵗʰ	Dull to fine. High S.W. wind. Still Guns though up well – Infantry portions of A echelons not D.B.C. to be attached to us to learn the front. –	

S/ Marshall Lay R/H L
Comdg 2-S.A.C.

2nd DIVISIONAL AMMUNITION COLUMN.

J U L Y

1 9 1 6

CONFIDENTIAL

Hd. 2ND DIVISION
"Q" BRANCH
31 AUG. 1916
No. Q5603/4

D. A. G.,
3rd Echelon
 B A S E

Reference your C.R. No.140/452, dated 24th August, 1916.

Herewith War Diary of 2nd D.A.C., for July, 1916.

H.Q., 2nd Division.
31st August, 1916.

S P Dickinson Capt.
for Major General,
Commanding 2nd Division.

Page 1.

Army Form C. 2118.

Instructions regarding War Diaries and Intelligence Summaries are contained in F. S. Regs., Part II. and the Staff Manual respectively. Title pages will be prepared in manuscript.

WAR DIARY or INTELLIGENCE SUMMARY.

(Erase heading not required.)

VOL VIII 2nd Divisional Ammunition Column.
1916. July 1916.

Place	Date	Hour	Summary of Events and Information	Remarks and references to Appendices
CAUCOURT	1-7-16		Fine - Bombardment going on.	
	2nd		Fine - cooler. Sent 16 Drivers, 60 Gunners to batteries - Very heavy bombardment during night - Advance reported on SOMME - Major CUSHEN struck off strength -	
	3rd		Fine - Ammunition to be issued according to scale.	
	4th		Wet - Heavy storms.	
	5th		Changeable - Wet.	
	6th		Dull - Fair - 12 Drivers, 3 Gunners from Base arrived.	
	7th		Dull - Wet - Lines getting very bad - N.T.C. reported poisonous in pits of 4.5" Howitzers	
	8th		Wet to Fine - Lines drying - G.O.C., R.A. IVth Corps came round to inspect - satisfactory.	
	9th		Fine - 2nd Lieut. Thomas sent up to Trench Mortars - 2nd Lieut. MEADE to Corps Signals.	
	10th		Fair - Windy.	
	11th		Fair - Wind.	
	12th		Dull - Slight showers - G.O.C. 2nd Division inspected Column in lines - 36 men joined from Base - 23 Gunners 12 Drivers, 1 Fitter, 2 Officers - 2nd Lieut.EMERY and 2nd Lieut.EDWARDS - posted to No. 1 Section.	
	13th		Dull - Cold - Sent up 2 N.C.O's, 6 Gunners, 5 Drivers to Brigades also 1 Fitter.	

Page 2.

Army Form C. 2118.

WAR DIARY
or
INTELLIGENCE SUMMARY. 2nd Divisional Ammunition Column.
(Erase heading not required).

July 1916.

Instructions regarding War Diaries and Intelligence Vol. VIII
Summaries are contained in F.S. Regs., Part II. 1916.
and the Staff Manual respectively. Title pages (contd).
will be prepared in manuscript.

Place	Date	Hour	Summary of Events and Information	Remarks and references to Appendices
	July			
CAUCOURT	14th		Fair to Fine.	
,,	15th		Fine - D.D.R. 1st Army inspected horses for evacuation - Capt. FERNIE No. 3 Section promoted and ordered to 11th D.A.C. to Command. Left in afternoon. G.O.C. IVth Corps inspected No. 2 and 3 Sections.	
,,	16th		Dull to rain - 37th Division Artillery coming in - We closed up and put a Brigade on hill - 1 Section and M & S in village - 2 Sections in HERIPEE - Sent 16 Gunners, 12 Drivers, 2 Fitters up to Batteries.	
,,	17th		Very dull and misty. Rain.	
,,	18th		Dull to fine in evening - Handing over to 37th Division Artillery, T.M. Batteries.	
,,	19th		Fine - D.A. moved down to GAUCHIN Le GAL & CAUCOURT - Order to move by rail - 4 Drivers, 1 Trumpeter joined from Base.	
Moving	20th		Fine - D.A.C. began to move by 1/4 Sections each with a battery - Entraining during night and next day at BRYAS, PERNES and DIEVAL. Lieut. CHALMERS & THOMAS returned from T.M. Battery. Lieut. CORNAH, BURN-CALLANDER and Lieut. EWART joined from Base.	
by				
Rail.	21st		Headquarters and Details (S.A.A. Wagons) entrained at PERNES at 2 p.m. 11½ hours to entrain - and proceeded by train to LONGEREAU (AMIENS) - Arrived at 11 p.m., detrained by 1-30 a.m. -	

Page 3.

Army Form C. 2118.

WAR DIARY
or
INTELLIGENCE SUMMARY. 2nd Divisional Ammunition Column.
(Erase heading not required.)

July 1916.

Instructions regarding War Diaries and Intelligence Vol. VIII
Summaries are contained in F.S. Regs., Part II. 1916.
and the Staff Manual respectively. Title pages (contd).
will be prepared in manuscript.

Place	Date	Hour	Summary of Events and Information	Remarks and references to Appendices
CAUCOURT	July 21st		Marched 9 miles to VERQUEMONT.	
ECQUEMONT or DOUARS	22nd		Arrived in Camp by 4-50 a.m. - Come into XIII Corps Fourth Army - Camp much crowded in places	
	22nd		Owing to other formations and sections going to wrong places on ground. Fine.	
ECQUEMONT or DAOURS	23rd		Moved Infantry portion of Column to MORLANCOURT under Capt. PELHAM - Sent 5 Drivers to 41st Bde.	
,,	24th		Fine - Advanced portion moved to another position 3 miles E. of MORLANCOURT and 1½ miles N.W. of BRAY. - Rest of D.A.C. ordered to move to-morrow to BOIS DE TAILLES.	
BOIS DE TAILLES nr. RAY sur SOMME.	25th		Marched at 8 a.m. with Division Artillery - in at 1a.m. - Remounts arriving from Base at MERICOURT - Moved to Dump at CARNOY - Capt. PELHAM, 2nd Lieut. BOYD, 2nd Lt. WOLSEY, 2nd Lt. MEADE. - to near the Advanced Bomb and Grenade Dump. There is to be another more forward Dump, which later will be several Infantry Brigade Dumps - 34 men with the party - T.M.Btys. went up. - Draft of 12 Gunners 7 Drivers and 1 Fitter joined.	
BRAY	26th		Headquarters moved to Dump (gun ammunition and reserve S.A.A. and grenades) near BRAY. - sent 9 more men up to CARNOY Dump. - Took over 9th Division S.A.A. etc., also 3rd Division at BRAY Dump. - 1 Fitter joined. 1 Riding and 12 Mules 2 Horses L.D.	
,,	27th		Fine - Advanced D.A.C. moved back. - Several horses killed and wounded. - Took over Ammunition	

Page 4.

Army Form C. 2118.

WAR DIARY
or
INTELLIGENCE SUMMARY. 2nd Divisional Ammunition Column.

July 1916.

Instructions regarding War Diaries and Intelligence Vol. VIII
Summaries are contained in F.S. Regs., Part II. 1916.
and the Staff Manual respectively. Title pages (contd).
will be prepared in manuscript.   (Erase heading not required).

Place	Date.	Hour	Summary of Events and Information	Remarks and references to Appendices
BRAY	July 27th		Refilling Point Dump from 9th D.A.C. at 8 p.m. - 1 Fitter joined- Loading and receiving ammunition all night. A 7881, AX 1500, BX 2756.	
	28th		Fine - Busy all morning and rest of day returning ammunition 11350 and 14700 rounds Total A 19054, AX 4180, BX 5570.	
ar BRAY L.9.a.)	29th		Fine and hot. Water difficulty increased - only watering twice a day and bad water.	
	30th		Fine - Advanced D.A.C. heavily shelled in night- but no casualties - ~~only watering twice a day and bad water~~. - Moved to position further W. D.A.C. ordered to move near MEAULTE, but order cancelled in afternoon. Sent 11 gunners 16 drivers 1 trumpeter to batteries.	A AX BX 8177,2314,1464
MEAULTE	31st		Moved at 10 a.m. to ground E. of MEAULTE. Sections being S. of village. H.Q. and Dump E. A great improvement as water is ample for horses and convenient. Distances not much greater. 3 officers for T.M.Batteries. 2/Lt. WOLSEY, 2/Lt. EWART, and 2/Lt. BURN-CALLENDER, also 3 men. Fine and very hot. No. 87477 Dr. E. Bushaway and No. 102,903 Dr. P. Hardy wounded that day.	6350,910, Nil

(sd) St J Du Plat Taylor, Lt.Col.
Comdg. 2nd D.A.C.

July 31st, 1916.

2nd Divisional Artillery

2nd DIVISIONAL AMMUNITION COLUMN R.F.A.

AUGUST *and September* 1916

WAR DIARY
or
INTELLIGENCE SUMMARY.
(Erase heading not required.)

Army Form C. 2118.

Vol IX
August 1916

2nd Div.l Am.n Col.

Vol 25

Place	Date	Hour	Summary of Events and Information	Remarks and references to Appendices
MEAULTE	Aug 1st		Fine - v. hot. 2 Lt Burn Callender. Working & Convoy to T.M. Batteries. here	Three /- AX. 13x.
			No 1 Sec to E. & No 3. on which way R E also to make room for ST. Gun	5282. 1600. 3176.
			Lt Burt posted to 41st Bde.	
	"	2nd	Fine. v. hot. 35 Bde AC. 1st Sec. & B Echelon arrived the attached. Took over 3"	3133, 3678. 1218
			Gun Amm. Dump. 35 Bolton No 2. Section killed in action being night.	
			Supply of 35 Bm Matheirses & was up the 3rd Siv Dump. —	
	"	3rd	Fine. R.A. moved the heavy T.M. bombs under cover of day out in old Sap Battery, a large	6746. 2268. 3696.
			supply of Amn coming up."	
	"	4th	Fine. Cooler & keep it. M. Rennantt arrived at 3.20 p.m from Base. 8 Gunners & 3170	3249 1226
			Be Hebird fragments returning — 2 men to R.R. Course to A. Batty A.A...	
	"	5th	Cooler. Fine. Supply of Mind Dump with Pelham McCurlin being well with his men.	
			Dump reported invisible by observations in hut at about 2500 ft. —	2976. 3745. 840
	"	6th	Cool & fine. Shells falling in neighborhood of Dump during night. Dump getting very large.	1642. 3170. 573
			an early day in unions.	
	"	7th	C G S to fine. V.E Dewar joined. Lt French to 23rd B. A.C. in Exchange with Lt Sim. 1/2 T.M. Artillery	
			Came in — attacked to NCH. —	1908. 3333. 992

WAR DIARY
or
INTELLIGENCE SUMMARY.
(Erase heading not required.)

Army Form C. 2118.

Vol IX
August 1916.

2nd Div. Amm. Col.

Place	Date	Hour	Summary of Events and Information	Remarks and references to Appendices
MEAULTE	8th		Fine cold night. Later in morning cancelled. Heavy firing & fighting on the right. Enemy A.	Series. Ax. B×. 9895, 4804, 3638
			in all night & during the day. Some of horses attached to 101st are feeling it much.	
			Ordered all units to be changed before they are really run down.	
〃	9th		Fine v. hot. Enabled to fill some demands A.K, & 1st moving East. Capt.	
			Pelham & Adj. D.A.C. came out in afternoon. 26 Remounts to 1st came	
			in also. Draft of 10 Drivers joined from base. Q. Harrison[?] wounded accidentally. 10,082. 2636. 68.	
〃	10th		Dull, slight rain. Various orders re moving. Sept 9. 15 gun fired from	5696, 2358, 2200
			base. A.M. to King posted to lines.	562 AP
〃	11th		Dull, hot, misty. Preparing a new A.R.P. for 2nd Div., present one to be handed over	
			to 24 DAC Tournes. Supplied Echelons into Dump, when orders came R. 8890, 3022, 2655.	
			fell up again with S.A.A. Capt. Maclean joined from old 3rd D.A.C.	
w/ MEAULTE	12		Dull fine - very hot. Moved HQtrs to W.7 Section. Handed over Dumps R.24 - D.A.C at 12 noon.	
			& arranged over the amm. main dumps about 1/2 m back. Much delay due t 35 Div	
			not sending in own Amm. till 12-30. During call of telephone wires[?] with	2332. 1818. 684
			withdraw H.Q. in no time. Direct[?] wires with H.Q. S.O. Subsistered around EGo	
			to units much. [illegible] [illegible] [illegible] much yours[?] [illegible]	
			on 14th to am Efoy.	

WAR DIARY or INTELLIGENCE SUMMARY

Army Form C. 2118.

Vol IX
2nd Div. Aus. Col.
Aug. 1916.

Place	Date	Hour	Summary of Events and Information	Remarks and references to Appendices
MEAULTE	13th		Rain & fine cooler.	H. Ax. Bx.
"	14th		Moved office & staff to near Dumpes. SAA section of A & B echelon left under Capt. Pelham by march route for BELLOY via VECQUEMONT & AYLERS. Dep[ot] 3832, 2204, 384. A1 Smokes, 15 gal[lons] petrol from stores.	114. 1152. 804
"	15th		Dull & rainy, 24 Bn Clamand for Amt.	3147. 2752. 1352
"	16th		Fine & fine. Moved H.Q. to near Dumps, no Dumpers out of branch. Capt H.T. BELLEVILLE joined, posted to No. 3 but is not competent to command it.	3796. 716. 334
"	17th		Showery. Sent party to St SAUVEUR to remount. SAA section moving to BUS. LES ARTOIS. ?	6052. 1380. 1776
"	18th		Cooler & showery. Amm. nearly all out at 6 p.m. arranged to assist with Bn echelon in next 12 hours if there is a rush on.	3224. 16. 1804
"	19th		Showery, cool. Group very empty. Amm. MT cars in night had to be Dumped near main road owing to enemy state of Amm. Dep[ot]	6742 · 374 · 2856
"	20th		Windy & cool. All Amm. Gens out & evening	D[riv]r Kelly wounded K
"	21st		Fine. Air raid by German planes, no bombs nearer than next camp. T.M. batteries left for COIGNEUX, M²E for fully recognize as per the HEDAUVILLE Road ???	5723 - 1150

T2134. Wt. W708-776. 500000. 4/16. Sir J.C. & S.

WAR DIARY
or
INTELLIGENCE SUMMARY

Army Form C. 2118.

Vol. IX
August 1916

2nd Div. A. Col.

Place	Date	Hour	Summary of Events and Information	Remarks and references to Appendices
MEAULTE	22nd	—	Fair — closing up dumps & preparing to move. 2/Lt Haven, Haley, Scott & Trapp joined. Drafts to Nos 2, 1, 3 & 4 Secs. Draft of 68 gnrs & 17 drivers from Base.	
t Bois de TAILLES	23rd	—	Fair to wet in afternoon. Filled up & handed over balance of Dumps to 6th D.A.C. who came on to be formed. Moved to BOIS de TAILLES at 10 am. Section morning at 8.30 am. Sent 16 gnrs 21 drs to Batteries.	
VECQUEMONT	24th		Marched at 4.30 pm to VECQUEMONT in bivouac at 10 p.m. 12 miles.	
ALLONVILLE	25th		Marched to ALLONVILLE at 3.15 pm in to bivouac at 6.30 p.m. 8 miles.	
SARTON	26th		Marched at 8.30 am via RUBEMPRE - BOCAGE, TALMAS, BEAUQUESNES, to SARTON. In to Billets at 4.45 pm. 20m. fair, heavy shower. —	
—	27th		(Rest & mild). Sent & greets 2/Lt Insley, Scott, Jackson, Trapp & Brydes, also 20 L.D. Knew. to have open front at nights.	
COIGNEUX & S LEGER	28th		Marched at 9.30 am for bivouac at St LEGER. H.Q. going to Dump at COIGNEUX & Park Dumps to be opened as arranged by Corps. Took over from Cav Div Arty.	
"	29th		Lt. Sections moved to bivouac near St LEGER. Advanced section to be kept entirely separate, Capt Pelham commanding it.	

Army Form C. 2118.

WAR DIARY
or
INTELLIGENCE SUMMARY.
(Erase heading not required.)

Vol IX
August 1916
2nd I.A.C.

Place	Date	Hour	Summary of Events and Information	Remarks and references to Appendices
COIGNEUX	30th		Very wet. No anumunition received rd Dump yet. 30 H.S. T.M. bombs moved from old "Dump" & Dump & store 18pr & 4.5 How amm —	
"	31st		Fine – Grand Dump. complete. G.O.C. & Capts RA came here Dump. Arranged t move H.Q. ST LEGER to AUTHIE.	

Sgd. A.H.Hay Style
Lt Col.

Army Form C. 2118.

WAR DIARY
or
INTELLIGENCE SUMMARY.
(Erase heading not required.)

VOL X   2' S.A.C.
Sept. 1916   VOL X

Place	Date	Hour	Summary of Events and Information	Remarks and references to Appendices
ST LEGER	1st		Fair. Gale. Moved A.Q. to ST LEGER on more central. Ammn received during night from Park. Some 2" T.M. bombs from Old S.A.C. Supn. not at Dump rendr. —	
"	2nd		26 O.R's joined from Base —	
"	3rd		Fine. Routine. —	
"	4th		Fair. Routine —	
"	5th		Wet after noon. Arranging lines for hutting site.	
"	6th		Very wet. Routine — 16 gph rain prevents game from same.	
"	7th		Fine — Drying up. 52 Reinforcements for Divn. some for S.A.C.	
"	8th		Fine — routine.	
"	9th		Fair — routine.	
"	9th		Fine — Dump A.R.P. & lifts to transportation. Repairing trackwheel. Unarmy rifle &c.	
"	10th		Fine — completing shifts of A.R.P. Work on Lotos Rivet & trophies. — 8 Offr. joined at night	
"			T/Capt. Gronde parties to So.Mally. — S. Partn. into S.S.A.C. — 319 r. parts & supplies	
"	11th		Fine. 6 officers posted & sent to Brigades. T.M. Batteries.	
"	12th		Fine. Supply of 2" & 114 Brim 10 gr. 2 batsmts (5th + 1 Sept) from same. Completed	
"			about Damaged HE cartridges	

Army Form C. 2118.

WAR DIARY or INTELLIGENCE SUMMARY.

Vol X   **2nd S.A.Bde.**
Sept '16

(Erase heading not required.)

Instructions regarding War Diaries and Intelligence Summaries are contained in F.S. Regs., Part II. and the Staff Manual respectively. Title pages will be prepared in manuscript.

Place	Date	Hour	Summary of Events and Information	Remarks and references to Appendices
ST LEGER LES AUTHIE	13th		Usual Routine. 12 wagons & rest of 9th Battery at night.	
"	14th		Fine, cold. Routine.	
"	15th		Fine - cold. Routine.	
"	16th		Afternoon cold. Routine. 24 men to Fenvillers.	
"	17th		Fine warmer. B.D.R. Res Army came round in morning.	
"	18th		Gale of wind & rain all day. Lifted up 6 S. wagons to carry water, made frame of wood with stretchers across & removed all unnecessary fire in a few minutes, wagon covers on water bag & covers. Inspected by Brig & funnel. 15 kh fitted up in S.A.C.	
"	19th		Fine & fine - cold. Draft 27 O.R. 50 G.S. from base.	
"	20th		Cold. Tech. Routine.	
"	21st		Fair - 3 Off. Dr. to Brigades. By Remounts came from Div. orders at night for 2 A echelon sections on foot & A echelon to go with Brigades to II Corps tomorrow. Lt Hollaman Rollins & auct's — TM [indistinct]	
"	22nd		Fine Hostilities remounts. 15 A.A. guns (nations 1 & 3) wagons left under Capt Pulhman & to leave TM [indistinct] not ??? as ??? about Inspection of B echelon wagons.	
"	23rd		Fine. B. echelon S.A.A. wagons returned from adv. S.A.C. Capt McBellonville orders to base.	

T2134. Wt. W708–776. 500000. 4/15. Sir J. C. & S.

WAR DIARY
or
INTELLIGENCE SUMMARY.
(Erase heading not required.)

Vol X
Sept 1916
2nd S.A. Col[?]

Army Form C. 2118.

Place	Date	Hour	Summary of Events and Information	Remarks and references to Appendices
ST LEGER LES AUTHIE	24"		Fine, routine. 2/Lt O'Brien proceed on leave till 4th Oct. 2/Lt Prowse to the Depot. — Capt Prowse & 2/Lt Phillips & 2/Lt [?] joined. N°3, 2/Lt Miller N°1, 2/Lt Stephen N°2, 2/Lt Brown [?] N°4 [?]	
	25"		Fine routine. Capt Melville left for France.	
	26"		V. Fine. Heavy wind of T.M. bombs point to S.M. [?] attempted & piled up ready to [?] [?] Capt Pelham. So many detachments & Dumps it makes [?] & security of [?] [?] [?] to consideration.	
	27"		Fine — Routine	
	28"		Fine — 2/Lt Cooke [?] [?] from T.M. Batteries. A Pty of 51st Div. [?] the N°4 Section 2/Lt Stephen and 10 men taken up to T.M. Batteries.	
	29"		Wet, routine. L/Cpl Ford our A.R.C. on Crunch & his [?]	
	30"		Fine - Rain at night, took it [?] have been [?] stopped is now of [?] more material also [?] & get [?] routine. [?] [?]	

2nd Divisional Artilery

2nd DIVISIONAL AMMUNITION COLUMN R. F. A.

OCTOBER 1916.

WAR DIARY or INTELLIGENCE SUMMARY

Army Form C. 2118

2nd Inf'n Bde
Vol XI October 1916

Vol 27

Place	Date	Hour	Summary of Events and Information	Remarks and references to Appendices
ST LEGER	1st	1 am	Change of time to normal. Fine. Routine.	
LES AUTHIE	2nd		From RVO2 int Gen. Vol. Bde gave lecture for the S. Company/General Every Day to S.O.s/Batt's & A.R.F.	
"	3rd		Changeable – arriving men FSMQ Bus – to camp on hillage SKT54/ ARIL 4 Colman Bus. 41 men arrived from base at night.	
Bucquoy W. Bus	4th		Wet – moved out into camp on high ground S. of Bus.	
"	5th		Rain. Reliefs sent for Bus. 3 Officers sent to 41st Bn. 2 Officers to 36th Bn. Lt Col Boys returned from Lieut Terbie's Genl Assistant's duties. Detachments from 36th & 41st Brigades from II Corps.	
"	6th		Fair. Sir B. Nelson returned with 36th & 41st Brigades from II Corps.	
"	7th		Fair – Visit present at Battalion of Br Birkbeck & Turney ARF's each Officer to Military to take charge of Inchony in certainly release the way to SO. operation at Tangle close to Colman.	
"	7th		Rain. Very March in of Division. Att present at Relieve change of Reserve battery.	
Bucquoy NE Bus	8th		Very wet. Practically all day. Moved into billets North East of Bus. Very wet. Lt col to new attending on Trichlefield	

WAR DIARY
INTELLIGENCE SUMMARY

Army Form C. 2118.

Vol XI
October 1916
VOL XII

2nd D A COL.

Place	Date	Hour	Summary of Events and Information	Remarks and references to Appendices
Bivouac N.E. Bus	9th		Fine, bright day – 3rd Div Tot. Art. Colours ARP – 19th Div Tot. over Enemy ARP active	
"	10th		Fine. Brilliant sunshine and chief of Staff informed us his counterbattery was chief of plotter target. Arrangements so no battery central of plotter target	
"	11th		A/Helen. 2nd & 3rd Sections left 5.30pm. 7th Bde RHA and 6th Sections in morning men between. Inspection of horses & AD Veterinary	
"	12th		Show – Capt gave orders from Base B. 36 Sec 15 Vet NCO Police.	
"	13th		Vay – isles. Capt B's 2 spooled plan Bde Routine.	
"	14th		Concentr. Capt. B. 27 Bd 16 cho 2 Tumplow 2 ammunition & Brigade	
"	15th		Fine, warm & dry. Enemy heavy ammunition a large hostile heavy return shoot by 10 Mid. Art Sec Car & casual 5 in action, returned broken submitted to RA – Thomas waited L/Cpl du Plat Taylor returned from leave	
"	16th		C.B. from Routine. SAA Section moved to new position between BEAUSSART & FORCE-VILLE	
"	17th		Heavy rain & gale at night – thunderstorm 1000 hoses of 3rd Adjutant & had men away & water difficulties. Lt O'Brien Nt Command No 3 Sec. 2/Lt headed Lt A/Pl.	

WAR DIARY or INTELLIGENCE SUMMARY.

Army Form C. 2118.

Instructions regarding War Diaries and Intelligence Summaries are contained in F.S. Regs., Part II. and the Staff Manual respectively. Title pages will be prepared in manuscript.

Vol XI   2nd Div. Am. Col.   Oct 1916

Place	Date	Hour	Summary of Events and Information	Remarks and references to Appendices
½ mile N.E. of BUS	18		Wet & windy all day. Lines & convoys getting very bad. Sent off party & horses for bean.	
	19		Area THIEVRES. Wet during night & heavy rain & wind all day. Lines very bad. Considerable trouble in arrangements of rear party. Carried for Am. Infantry regiment to most improvise - material nil -	
	20		Snow, very cold N.E. wind all day. A try on scanty lines & men. Pathy since insp. Hard frost at night & threats will be necessary.	
	21		Fine, but roads wind after frost. Some rich beginning. Remounts to arrive strength for Sup.	
	22		Fine after hard frost at night, cold wind of S.E. wind home remounts to sub 300 2nd D.A. to front in swamp.	
	23		Fog, most of day, milder. To Div. Arty & A.R.P. a lot of Amm. coming in hard 20 in the head of men - took them about more than can be coopeted with no upds. supplies, should we use sending to brigades of 49th Div. demanded better blankets for men.	
	24		Very wet all night - continued all day. Ground around a bog of mud.	
	25		Very long work of day - 21 breaks posted to 70th Battery. #27 Gp. 18 Gr fr 1 other Div. Tipp from horse.	

WAR DIARY or INTELLIGENCE SUMMARY

Army Form C. 2118.

VOL XI 2nd D.A.C.
October 1915

Place	Date	Hour	Summary of Events and Information	Remarks and references to Appendices
½ mile N.E. of B.W.S.	26th		Weather improving — cleared in afternoon. Extra 50 men sent to A.R.P. & clean up the Shed. led became transport. 9 men for 2nd Canadian Divn arrived at night. There is a constant confusion in letters &c every second Canadian being omitted. —	
	27th		Heavy rain — Reld. pole all day. Operations part of organising its being arranged in front area.	
	28th		Rain and sleet for a Col during day.	
	29th		Snow & rain — very bad on horses. Given 16 gun, 16 Dr., 1 fitter, 1 S.S. & 4 rydrs. A.R.P. to be moved to higher ground.	
	30th		Snow to a & depth & rain in aft. A new scheme for employing men & batteries started — if it succeeds I will have an immense lot of men & horses at work. —	
	31st		Fine — snow beginning to dry.	

Stanley May/ Lt Col
Comdg 2. D.A.C.

2nd Divisional Artillery.

2ND DIVISIONAL AMMUNITION COLUMN R.F.A.

DECEMBER 1916.

Army Form C. 2118.

WAR DIARY
or
INTELLIGENCE SUMMARY.

VOL XIII   2nd Div. Am. Col.
Dec. 1916

Vol 29

(Erase heading not required.)

Place	Date	Hour	Summary of Events and Information	Remarks and references to Appendices
BUS.	1st	—	Frost. Quiet. Handing over A.R.P's closing and account to Batty on our area. Came up. 45 ppr. reinforcements from base. Sent 10 Klak. axles & 5 T.Ms Batteries. 5 remount in S.A.C.	
AMPLIER	2nd		Marched at 12 noon to AMPLIER via BUS & SARTON. Fine, bright day - Dull that 3 p.m. Very comfy billets.	
HEIRMONT	3rd		Cold & foggy. Marched at 10 am for HIERMONT via DOULLENS (18 miles). Delay of half an hour by Brigade in front. In at billets at 4.50 pm. Sup. again full - but were two yesterdays. Supplied not in till 8.30 pm.	
FROYELLES	4th		Fost. clear. Reconnoitred FROYELLES & CUMONVILLE. Tender fir power (road) held H.Q. & In. Gs. Nos 1,2 & 4 sent over there. On receipt of report on CUMONVILLE decided to send No4 there tomorrow. No3 & Hd-am at HEIRMONT. Sea low in very L.T. —	
	5th		Under rain & fog in trenches. Sent No4 T.O. to CUMONVILLE morning. Capt Harlean returned from leave —	
	6th		Pontine. Getting in to billets. 32 Remount collected from S'RIQUIER Sta. —	

Army Form C. 2118.

WAR DIARY
or
INTELLIGENCE SUMMARY.

(Erase heading not required.)

2 - D. A. C.

Vol XIII
Dec. 1916

Place	Date	Hour	Summary of Events and Information	Remarks and references to Appendices
FRIEULLES	7.		Sent party to fetch Remounts from ABBEVILLE. 35 brought in. Out - fossy. —	
	8th		Wet - milder. D.D.V.S. Fifth Army came round. —	
	9th		Wet. 14 Drivers reinforcements from base. After discussion with D.A.Q.M.G. put up proposition for organisation & arrangement of D.A.C. & Div. Tps present system does not work as S.A. sections being D. Tps. lots led to a lot of trouble in administration etc. Ideal arrangement would be a separate S.A. section with proper staff & officers. B section officer to be superflous & R.G. portion of D.A.C. handed) to better organise) as D.A.C. (H.Q. of D.A.C. is to be superfluity & only an extra expense in officers, N.C.O.s, horses & carriages. Staff Capt. does & can run the Ammn. train this officer if necessary under him for Ammn. work would) meet the urgent demand. —	
	10th		Fair to wet. nowt true. — Send him to Col. Thomas for Farrier Sgt.	
	11		Fine - cold. Broke up S.A. sections to reorganise old each section to act apt —	

Army Form C. 2118.

WAR DIARY
or
INTELLIGENCE SUMMARY.

Vol XIII 2" D.A.C.
Dec 1916

(Erase heading not required.)

Instructions regarding War Diaries and Intelligence Summaries are contained in F. S. Regs., Part II. and the Staff Manual respectively. Title pages will be prepared in manuscript.

Place	Date	Hour	Summary of Events and Information	Remarks and references to Appendices
TROYELLES	Dec 12 Tuesday		Snow & rest. Fatigues & routine —	
	13ʳᵈ		Cold. Gen. G.S.C came round — routine	
	14ᵗʰ		Routine (cold)	
	15ᵗʰ		v. wet all day. G.O.C. 2ⁿᵈ Div. came round. German peace proposals —	
	16ᵗʰ		fine v. cold wind. 2ⁿᵈ reliefs — (Lt. Tucker joined from base —	
	17ᵗʰ		foggy. cold. routine.	
	18ᵗʰ		Cold — routine.	
	19ᵗʰ		cold. misty routine —	
	20ᵗʰ		Frost — fine. 80 men found from base — 35 Gp. & 29 Bm —	
	21ˢᵗ		Heavy gale f. S.W.	
	22ⁿᵈ		Wet & milder —	
	23ʳᵈ		mild. v. heavy gale f. S.W. — routine.	
	24ᵗʰ		fine — mild. Arranged reorganisation within Div. of Sections	8 photographs
			see App. I. It is only a makeshift, but is a practicable foundation for a permanent	App I —
			organization. — 20 Gp. 34 Bm sent to Ariples.	
	25ᵗʰ		fair, hard wind. Routine —	

T2134. Wt. W708—776. 500000. 4/15. Sir J. C. & g.

Army Form C. 2118.

WAR DIARY
or
INTELLIGENCE SUMMARY.

2" D.A.C.

VOL XIII
Dec. 1916

(Erase heading not required.)

Instructions regarding War Diaries and Intelligence Summaries are contained in F.S. Regs., Part II. and the Staff Manual respectively. Title pages will be prepared in manuscript.

Place	Date	Hour	Summary of Events and Information	Remarks and references to Appendices
FROYELLES District	26th		Routine. Point to work. Draft of 1 S/Sgt (& SMC) 18 Dr. 51 Gnr. joined from Base.	
	27th		Cold, fine. 78 Reinforcements (mules) joined from Adv MT Depot. Lt. Ralston Scott of N. Horse joined, to look after bathing mojor lines.	
	28th		Hard frost, fine. Drill. Routine.	
	29th		Still mild. Had visit GOC II Corps. Inspected billets at HEBUTERNE, also GOC 2" Div.	
	30th		Thaw, showery. Had visit (exchange) 47 mules which had had incomplete sore backs for 47 fit from A.H.T.D.	
	31st		Lawn mild. 26 Gnrs 13 B.d" to Brigades, also 40 L.D. Horses.	

S/ Frank Long Pal Col
Comdg 2" D.A.C.

Vol XIII
2ND DIVL. AMMUN. COL.

San Diery App. I

H.Q.2ND DIVL AMMN. COL.
29 DEC. 1916
R.F.A.

	Officers	Deno H.O.	Deno H.O.	Staff Sgt.	Sergeants	Corporals	Bombardiers	Gunners	Drivers	Saddlers	Shoeing Smiths	Fitters	Wheelwrights	Trumpeters	Artificer Ceno M.O.	Drivers	Gunners	Batmen	Lukers	Total	Drivers	Gunners	B. ?	Total	4 horses	4.5 Waggons	18 pdr A. Waggons	4.5 Am. Waggons	Motor Lorries	Bicycles
H.Q.	2	1		1	4	4			15	1					3			14	5	21	29	3	3	28	36	3				2	2
S.A.A. 1	4			7	4	4	5		18	4			4	1	2	1		157	4		237	4	17	307	338	1	12		2	2	
2	2			1	4	4	5	1	22	4	1	1	4	1	2	1		62	2		131	2	17	112	131	1	12	4			3
3	3			1	4	4	5	1	14	6	1	1	4	1	2	2		80	3		157	3	17	151	171	1	18	4			3
4	4			1	6	4	7	1	22	4	1	1	4	1	3	5		160	4		264	4	18	322	344	2	18	4		1	3
Total	15	1		5	18	18	22	4	74	18	4	4	15	4	9	9		479	18	2	817	18	72	920	1010	7	15	18	12	2	3	14

The above establishment includes 7 Sergts. & Sr. for 1, 2, & 3 Sections, 1 for Std Qtr.
9 Shoe & 15 Shoe for 1, 2, 3 & 4 Sections.
7 Bicycles will be for HQ & Bat. Sections (attached), Riders for these from men included in the above establishment.

In addition to the above N.C.O from B (-) 2 & 3 Sections will be used for Remps. Any remnants N.C.O from C.

2nd Divisional Artillery

2ND DIVISIONAL AMMUNITION COLUMN R.F.A.

NOVEMBER 1916

Army Form C. 2118.

WAR DIARY
or
INTELLIGENCE SUMMARY.
(Erase heading not required.)

November 1916.
2nd Div. Am. Col.
Vol XII
Nov. 1916.

Vol 28

Place	Date	Hour	Summary of Events and Information	Remarks and references to Appendices
N.E. of BUS	1st		Fair - land still drying in spite of rain. Horse lines steadily tend to Red area.	
	2nd		Fair after rain in a.m. No 27,351 Dr/ Durbin & No 64,065 Dr/ Isard received commendation for gallant original under fire on 20th Oct. 1916. This action has been reported to Bve Brigade. Anyone working with horse lines may have time to sort from team area. No 2 Sec. & Co for one a about 20 from other lines tether 120 from S.A.A.	
	3rd		Fine - land drying hard between. 60 lines/mules of D.A.C. sent back who 340 from Myadle (mostly St. E. lines) D.A.C. is now no better than if he would be wiser to will take some time to get mules after again	
	4th		Fine to wet again. Lines & land getting bad. 12h Reinforcements Dr. at night.	
	5th		Gale & some rain. Storms renewed.	
BUS	6th		Showery + hard H.Q. in to Road for shelter & to get out of mud.	
	7th		Heavy rain + hail all day. Horse and lines are getting deep near 22 9"-21 8"- 1 Pun G.	
			Filter arrived from Arras	
	8th		Fair to showers. Draft came in from Rouilbad. Fresh intense to be worked.	
	9th		Fine + bright - strong before + drying up + refit & work mules lines	

T2134. Wt. W708-776. 500000. 4/15. Sir J.C.&S.

WAR DIARY
or
INTELLIGENCE SUMMARY

Army Form C. 2118.

Vol XII 2nd S.A.C.
November 1916

Place	Date	Hour	Summary of Events and Information	Remarks and references to Appendices
BUS	10th		Fine — routine	
	11th		Dull & foggy — operations being prepared for.	
	12th		Fine, mild. Drying up well. Bombardment all day, completely enveloped. Issued 20 boxes to Brit. regiments. 15 gun 3 S.S. —	
	13th		Fair, misty. Bombardment began at dawn — Mr Collins wounded at night.	
	14th		Fine, dull. Heavy fighting & many prisoners again coming in. A.R.C very busy all night & day. It is hoped the breeze with the bad roads & shell fire?	
	15th		Fair — Snee und & cells in the E. Ammunition supply still very heavy. —	
	16th		Had first fine & S.A.A. section to do all with lepathy, down letter a nothing in A.T.C. —	
	17th		Frost, cold. E wind. Park of S.A.A. left — out & fellow tomorrow. —	
	18th		Frost, snow at night, in morning. Park of S.A.A. left. 10 men & T.M's & 19th Bdee, thru r. Scene army of S.A.A. + A.R.C.	
	19th		Snoden wind in S.S.W. Heavy rain at night. Have [illegible] to travel with md/fm.!	
	20th		Snow S.W wind. Drying, moving S.A.A. which has been dumped by sections where they wanted on 18th..	

WAR DIARY
or
INTELLIGENCE SUMMARY.

Army Form C. 2118.

VOL XII   2nd D.A.C.
November 1916

Place	Date	Hour	Summary of Events and Information	Remarks and references to Appendices
B.U.S.	21st		Cold - fog all day. Routine	
	22nd		Frost. Clear - Routine. Leave opened 9 O's & R. every week for B.A.C.	
	23rd		Cold - Frost. Routine.	
	24th		Rain & milder. Draft 25 men came from Base. 18 NCO's & 7 Gnrs	
	25		Heavy gale of wind & rain - roads in a bad state.	
	26		Rain till 11:0. Then cleared. Sent 12 Gnrs & 8 O's up to Brigades.	
	27		Gales, frosty, clear & moving cancelled.	
	28		" Routine rejoining A Wheelers. Staff are up to all below up and impossible to get any returns in.	
	29		Cold - dull. An accident at A.R.P. in moving a round of HE exploded, killed only Sher 1 up & Gnrs. & injuring 4 others, body wounded 3 men including gp Binns of Dte Artilery & one or nearby another, they recovered a Cndy of Young Ret'd Draft of 1 St & 15 gnrs from Base. 58 miles from no Demanche.	
	30		Cold - dull. Also used needed in moving to go out on 2nd Regt. Supt in Ablaine rare after.	

S Punchfield Majr ... Col
Comdg 2/DAC

2ND DIVISION
ROYAL ARTILLERY

2ND DIVL AMMUNITION COLUMN.

JAN-DEC 1917

2nd Divisional Artillery.

2nd DIVISIONAL AMMUNITION COLUMN R.F.A.

JANUARY 1917.

WAR DIARY or INTELLIGENCE SUMMARY

Army Form C. 2118

Vol I 2d S.A.C.
January 1917

Place	Date	Hour	Summary of Events and Information	Remarks and references to Appendices
FROYELLES	1st		Train milk to rest stop routine.	
OCCOCHES	2		Train milk left at 9 am - picked up other section via LE PONCHEL & AUXI-LE CHATEAU to billet in OCCOCHES 2.1 m.m.	
MARIEUX & AMPLIER	3rd		Hd md & met md marched at 11·0 am for MARIEUX (H.Q. Nos 4 & 2) AMPLIER Nos 3 & 1.	
BOUZINCOURT SENLIS	4th		Very wet. marched at 9 am for SENLIS BOUZINCOURT. Billets house in open.	
"	5th		Fri v. cold. Routine.	
POUZINCOURT	6th		Moved to BOUZINCOURT after 51st Div. Took over A.R.P. at noon, from 51st Div. Lines & billets very dirty - had worked out not all in till late.	
"	7th		Took over S.A.M. — many stores from 51st. Rest at night - frosty day. Sapping in by AM's.	
"	8		Sevr. intermy. foncades myslf. generally cleaning up lines & billets. notting timely outflows & later. Get riffles 50 founded & later. febries HARE repting.	
"	9		...	

WAR DIARY
or
INTELLIGENCE SUMMARY.
(Erase heading not required.)

Army Form C. 2118

Vol I 2nd ANZAC

January 1917

Place	Date	Hour	Summary of Events and Information	Remarks and references to Appendices
Bayencourt	10		Dire Slight Frost. Some slaps of Relief RA & RE intercharges are reporting. A column alleged still up with an art but would feature at Coy G. Bois IV. F.S. made returned Dum Cops. It has paid to to inform 25th Div much crater slopes Spring Holland Force one adjutant Nylics Releivements arrived form the Base if 1 Bde 1 Sgt 13 Offr RA — RE/offrs 2 NCO's Casualty Umacilly Informer Billets times so various.	
"	11	"		
"	12	"	Gradually Brighter & Cold scene RA — RE l arms fatigues Offr Mary Tactical Duties) Relief to Sub Div. 2nd Australian returned to its 2 Bde from timespare May Mileages Withe evening It Alerysta spent Christch Capt Kirby	
"	13	"	Mercury + 2nd 32 made informer. Jnn with Caps. To had + 609 Mules Due RA — RE offrs sterlmp + 6 shs & ant to 36 Brigade 1 Trip to the 41st Brigade Traded of B.83. 18 Minoam Accommodation	
	14	"	Relieve was permitted to R T.	
	15	"	Dire Frost 50 arch art to 2nd Brit Pul to spend 5 O.J Monday for another future is marks with holders children. It Trestlepe Capt — Bit	

WAR DIARY or INTELLIGENCE SUMMARY

Army Form C. 2118

Vol - I
2nd D A C
January 1917

Place	Date	Hour	Summary of Events and Information	Remarks and references to Appendices
Bayencourt	16th		2 inches of snow - sent first 100 men fatigue parties. Same work except—	
"	17		part. 1 NCO & 12 men have been returned to 1st Div. 1 NCO & 12 men have been drawn from Nos 1, 2 & 3 sections to replace them at [Depot?] Not fatigue returns 2nd & 3rd wagons of 15th Battery 2nd & 3rd wagons D.16	
"	18		Snow all [in?] during the night. Parties to [mis?] [illeg] [illeg] that G.R.A. Returning. Capt Whitfield RAMC left BAC & Capt. Bear RAMC took over his duties [illeg] Lieut has ever acted as [illeg] her fatigue [carting?] [huttings?] material from Souil—and to [illeg]	
"	19		R A - R E Issued [illeg]	
"	20		R A - R E. Nothing [illeg] Staff from the Base of Reinforcement 1 Bdr. 3 Sergt (1 [illeg] for 36 [illeg] Bde)	
"	21st		Sent [illeg] nothing. [illeg] to 36 FBde 6 Sgts & others ([illeg] & [illeg] [illeg] typ Bde) [illeg] of [illeg] R.A. [illeg] 13 corps. 2nd Lieut [illeg] with 1 NCO + 12 [illeg] so men attached to 2nd D.A.C. to [illeg] it up. 1 NCO + 4 men attached to corps Gas Officer to be employed at Corps A.R.P. Demob Pool.	
"	22		Capt [illeg] Tredway and [illeg] [illeg] [illeg] [illeg] [illeg] from G. [illeg] & [illeg] to R.A. [illeg] [illeg]. Veterinary Officer [illeg] [illeg] returned from leave.	

WAR DIARY
or
INTELLIGENCE SUMMARY

Army Form C. 2118.

Vol. I 1917 2nd S.A.C.I.
January

Place	Date	Hour	Summary of Events and Information	Remarks and references to Appendices
BOUZINCOURT	23rd		Hud part - fine Routine - Capt Pelham went to 2nd Battn with 9 St Cpls	
	24th		ditto - ditto, commenced about Reorganization which present on form 25th	
	25th		Hud part - fine Reorganizing of SAC carried out Lieut no 2 Sn gone to 24th pln as Borg Lieut Clay army brigade under Capt Putnam 31 rank + kingston transferred to Near no 2 (Lieut no 3) Lieut also replan O.R. & horses + harnesses to 2 Spare sections of 2nd S.A.C. following O.R. transferred to B.A.C. if 446. 1 - Pttn. Mtt 1 - Vth 2 3 - Ferrier Wyd 1 - M3 - M2 - Bdr no 3 - Gun 35 - Dr 24 - Batman 1 - els 13 Riders 3 129 6	
	26th		White vest. 146 Mkmn 5 collected from Liberty tryl Hut - R+112 - other units 34. Brig Gent Hindle inspects Billets Litgas 1 in unit Next Doof W 1st H.g. 2d Lt 14 Pt Taylor OSO takes over Inspects A.V.B. Strallow of B34 Battery joined S.A.C as Ast FLItimt 16 Dr 3420	
	28th		Word Scent. 146 Offices from Base 112 SRA. 34 5 other units for true	

WAR DIARY
or
INTELLIGENCE SUMMARY.

Army Form C. 2118.

3rd D.A.C. Vol 30

Place	Date	Hour	Summary of Events and Information	Remarks and references to Appendices
Beaumont	29th		Marl. post gone over Lieut S.H. Mather (6 Field Ambulance) taken over medical charge of D.A.C. 2nd Lt H. Playfair transferred from 3rd to 2nd Sect. B. Echelon (R.A. Orders) 2nd Lt. F. Hughes posted to B. Echelon via 2nd Lt. B.C. Tucker to D 36 section.	
"	30th		Mafor post Capt F. Nunn AVC left for 34th I. Brigade 2nd Hand AVC	
"	31st		2nd Lt R. DAC. Lionel Galgano native Marl. post 2nd Lt W. Willis left from D 36 - native	

R Harlow Capt
Cmdg. 3rd DAC

2nd Divisional Artillery.

2nd DIVISIONAL AMMUNITION COLUMN R.F.A.

FEBRUARY 1917.

WAR DIARY or INTELLIGENCE SUMMARY

Army Form C. 2118.

Vol. 11 — 3rd A.C. — Vol. 31
February 1917

Place	Date	Hour	Summary of Events and Information	Remarks and references to Appendices
Bruaysement	1st		Wind front. The following N.C.O's and men were killed & wounded in the Advance of the A.R.P. Sunday Feb 1st:	
			0/6 2098 Cpl. Vigt. M.G. 4th Section — Killed	
			" 107221 L/Cpl Best R. " " — Killed	
			" 14743 L/Cpl Burgess G. 4th Section 0/6 123801 L/Cpl Murray C. 2nd Section Killed	
			" 135667 L/Cpl Gay E. 3rd Section 0/6 74827 " Saylor G. " " Killed	
			0/6 134917 Dr McCartney J. 2nd Section 16692 " Goodrich " " Killed	
			0/6 24226 Dr McMath J. 4th Section 23201 " Jones A. died of wounds	
			62549 Dr McPherson H. " " 0/6 27633 L/Cpl Ellis H. 4th Section	
			0/6 170242 Dr Murray J. 3rd Section 74628 L/Cpl Thomas S. 2nd Section Wounded	
			81767 Dr Murray E. " " Highly commended returned	
			Wind front. Round of fire and hostility fct. Taylor D.S.O. took charge	
		2nd	Not to detail. Wind front to England — nothing	
	3rd		Wed. Wind front. Very heavy fatigue — ration	
	4th		Men resting. It has been sent to assist II half of the A.R.P. fatigue — ration	
	5th		Wind front. No little running in A.R.P. duty — fatigues — ration	
			Wind front. No little running in A.R.P. duty to 20 central fatigue — ration	

WAR DIARY
or
INTELLIGENCE SUMMARY.

Army Form C. 2118.

Vol II
34 D A C
February 1917

Place	Date	Hour	Summary of Events and Information	Remarks and references to Appendices
Bouzincourt	6th		Hon. Dent. G.C.	2nd copls RA	CRA 2nd Div inspd	
"	7		Clothes, hair & teeth. usual fatigues — ration —	
"	8		Had Dept. out to reinforcement pm Bus — 1 Senior — 1 Writer — 4 Saddlers — 34 Gunrs — usual fatigues — ration —	
"	9		Maj. Dept 2nd Lieut Pinckford B.B. Echelon Company 1990 on pass the course of T.M.S. at Meleury — usual fatigues — ration —	
"	10		Had. Dept. usual fatigues — building station — ration —	
"	11		Hon. 2nd Lieut Mynn D.06.& Lieut Lepit. — General Coming 7 ration —	
"	12		Drft. Inspt. 2nd Lt. & Lt. 26 May tright + 7 & Men 13 2 Batts. inf'n Gunry 2nd Lt. Stephens and B.B. Echo. pm B.36.4 fatigues ration —	
"	13th		Strt for pm to Quench handed pm 1st Lt from D.36 —	
"	14		Weather rainy night + NY. 7 days. Cheek of the new boot Pickhaltons & reptd to Boo Sup. at Henry small fatigues. ration —	
"	15		Weather very bad + snow. 1 NCO & heard 1 Sgt 15 men & 1 Spt 6 men fatigues — ration —	

WAR DIARY or INTELLIGENCE SUMMARY

Army Form C. 2118.

Instructions regarding War Diaries and Intelligence Summaries are contained in F.S. Regs., Part II. and the Staff Manual respectively. Title pages will be prepared in manuscript.

Vol II 3rd D.A.C.

February 1917

Place	Date	Hour	Summary of Events and Information	Remarks and references to Appendices
Bray-sur-Somme	16		Snr. Sigual Fatigue - Routine	
"	17		Snr. Keny Fig. Towards Cerisy - Signal Fatigue - Routine	
"	18		Sun. Fatigue Remounts arrived. Bully Beefs Fatigue. Routine	
"	19		Records of Return reports to Staff Capt. R.A. Visits H.Q. Lines.	
"	20		Raining. Rides to Genl. Sandow. Visits No.3 X" & No.2 X" Sh Routine	
"	21		Muddy. Sunny morning. Visits No.1 X". Fatigues Routine	
"	22		Md. & night dry freezing rain. Inspects No.2 X". Fatigues Routine.	
"	23		Mildy. Fair. Inspects No.1 X". General routine Fatigues	
"	24		Bridy. Fair. Inspects H.Q. Lines. General routine Fatigues.	
"	25		Clear. Fair. Took action re erection of Road at Vecquemont Brit. W13.D.e. Gunners routine d.	
"	26		Clear. Fair. General Routine Fatigues etc. Inspects No.3 X".	
"	27		Windy. Fair. General Routine Fatigues.	
"	28		Clear Windy. Visits Dumps. General Routine Fatigues.	

Geo W Wight
Lt Col Cmdg 3rd DAC

2nd Divisional Artillery.

2nd DIVISIONAL AMMUNITION COLUMN R.F.A.

MARCH 1917.

Army Form C. 2118.

WAR DIARY
or
INTELLIGENCE SUMMARY.
(Erase heading not required.)

Vol II March 1917   2nd D.A.C   Vol 32

Place	Date	Hour	Summary of Events and Information	Remarks and references to Appendices
Bouzencourt	Wed. 1st		Brig.Lt. Survey. Visited & Inspected No 3 X" 2nd Grade & No 3 X" 6 Grade. General Fatigues. Rations.	
	2nd		Lowman Misty afternoon. Brig Lt. Inspected No 2 X". General Fatigues etc.	
	3rd		Dull. Saw Staff Capt". Re Advance of Stores + Au. W. Supply. Inspected Premises.	
	4th		Advanced Lines for Wagon of D.A.C. Water Supply + Hindrances. General Fatigues. Rations.	
	5th		Misty afternoon. General Fatigues. Rations. Strong E.S.E. Wind. Fair. Amount of Snow fell during night. Moving part of Chev. Inspected No 3 X". Rain. Vety Officer + NC. Returned - Park Accompanied. I.N.O. for 36 Bgde.	
	6th		8 men for R.A. Arsenals Line. 4 Subalterns for R.H. also reported & to Padres. No 2 + 3 X" Inspected. HQ DAC Lines. General Roches Fatigues.	
	7th		Fair. Visited S.A.H. Dumps. T. Dumps. 2 Subalterns arrived Y/OD.5/6 R.A.	
	8th		Fair. General Routine. General Fatigues.	
	9th		Misty + Dull. Visited S.A.A. Dumps. No 1 X" Lines. General Fatigues etc. Chev. Visited R.A.H.Q. ve. lifting our Div. Dumps. General Fatigues etc.	
	10th		His Lt. at P. Dumps ve General of same. 6 R.3.3.8.5. General Fatigues etc.	
	11th		Chev. A/Bright Snow Rain (SE/W) moving at R.33.d.5.5 (N Dump) Gen Fals + Rd etc.	
	12th		Chev. Rain during night. Qr. at N. Dump. General Fatigues etc.	

WAR DIARY or INTELLIGENCE SUMMARY.

Army Form C. 2118.

Vol II
2nd D.A.C.
March 1917

Place	Date	Hour	Summary of Events and Information	Remarks and references to Appendices
	13	Cloudy.	General fatigue. Inspection No III X" Trails & Dumps.	
	14	Clear.	Trails & Dumps. & Gun park. Vacated by Bgde. as used as Horse	
	15.	Cloudy.	Trails. R.A. H.Q. re moving and Gun pits. General Routine etc.	
	16	Misty.	Trails. Required Road Pits or Collecting Area etc. General Routine etc.	
	17	Brig. & Observ. at 16 Dumps. Trails P.O. & Collecting Area 16. General Routine etc.		
	18	Clear & Sunny.	No 2 & 3 X" Moved forward & M.T. Lorries. Trails Area 2, 3 X" General Routine etc.	
Vizers	19	Cloudy. Stormy. Wind. rain evening.	Trails. R.A. H.Q. re Collecting Area 16. Rougeoinet &	
		2 Officers & 25 O.R. arrived for 34th (B)de., & Dr. Jones from 2nd Div. General Routine ch.		
	20	Wet & Windy	At Dumps & Collecting Points for Area 16. Genl Routine etc.	
Bouzincourt	21	Cloudy.	At 16 Dumps & Collecting Points. Moved H.Q. D.A.C. to Bouzincourt. 7rd to 6.15 Genl.	
	22	Cloudy.	96th Lipon Munch. Col. Inspection 2 & 3 X" 5" Men opened from Puchevillen 9.2 Klin.	
	23	Fine.	80 horses loaned to Bgds. Collecting Amm'n & Dumping a X roads Warloncourt. Ulo 816	
	24	Fine.	Very cold. Strong winds. Moved pad from Bouzincourt, to Puche villes.	
Puche villes	25	Very & Sunny.	G.R.A inspected Gun line, Lines & Billets.	
	26	Rain & hail. Very cold.	Marched to Brio. Berges. H.Q. 2 & 3 X".	
B. Berges.	27.	Hail & Snow. Very cold.	Marched to Veil Heeden.	

Army Form C. 2118

WAR DIARY
or
INTELLIGENCE SUMMARY. 2nd D.A.C.

Vol II
March 1917

Place	Date	Hour	Summary of Events and Information	Remarks and references to Appendices
Neuf Berquin	28		Fine Windy. Snowstorm. Test Waders & Box respirators.	
	29		Rain later. Winds. Wagons cleaned, reharness, fatigues etc.	
	30		Rain & Hail. C.O. Marches to Stellervoit.	
	31		Rain. C.O. Marches to Gouy Servins.	
Gouy Servins				

W. Murphy Lt Col
Cmdg 2nd D.A.C

2nd Divisional Artillery.

2nd DIVISIONAL AMMUNITION COLUMN R.F. A

APRIL 1917.

WAR DIARY / INTELLIGENCE SUMMARY

Army Form C. 2118
Vol II
April 1917
2 D.A.C.
Vol 31

Place	Date	Hour	Summary of Events and Information	Remarks and references to Appendices
Gouy Servins	1st		Clear morning. Cold. Snow in afternoon. Interviews by 1st Canadian D.A.Q. re Remount Dumps. Location of Pack train. Genl Rankin. Fatigues.	
	2		Snow. Extremely cold wind. 3 Officers & 33 O.R. joined from Base. Horses apparently suffering much from the severe cold at R.H.Q. Rates Amt 643 Kts	
	3		Heavy snow. Moved all horses & mules including 4 Uncle? of Mr Packtrain to Winthrop Park totalling of Uncle?. Mr Packtrain to Winthrop Park. Packs Amt to 6 Bltns	
	4		Cloudy. Cold. 2 Officers & 3 N.C.O's detailed to go over trail for Pack Supply. 40 remounts arrived.	
	5		Xchanged 20 horses with No1. 10 per each No2 & 3 X's for mules. 3 Shellproof Boxes all near line. Clear. Quick warmer. Ambulance 40 remounts. 613/ hr for 13 Wks details to gunnery trail & at Post	
	6		Necessary Bridge repaired. Ammn Supply of SAA ordered. Supplied Ammn No 2 & 3 X's 6 Divn Post. Fair. Cloudy. At R.H.A. H.Q. with Lt Bellew re bridging and material necessary for trail. Several shells from enemy fell close Bivis. 2 horses killed. Moved 2 × 3 X's 6 new Bivis considerable shelling by enemy. In evening evening & night around Rankin's road. 4 X's	
	7		Clear. Strong NW wind. A light fall of snow during night. 6 & 7'' relieved 30 mules 6 SAA	
	8		Clear. Sunny. 20 mules to Rankin's dumps.	
	9		Snow falling during night. 10 mules to Summit Dumps. 2 Officers & 34 reinforcements arrived & Posts 6. 2 & 3 X's.	

Army Form C. 2118.

WAR DIARY
or INTELLIGENCE SUMMARY.
(Erase heading not required.)

Vol II 2 D.A.C.
April 1917.

Place	Date	Hour	Summary of Events and Information	Remarks and references to Appendices
Gouy Servins	10		Snow, rain, very cold. Inspected Sections 2 & 3. Saw O/C. P.T. vans at Tenure.	
	11		Strong wind. Snow. S.C.R.A. on move & supplying Tenure & B.H.Q.	
	12		Heavy Snow during night. Saw O/C Sections at Tenure for B.H.Q's provisional means.	
	13		Seen Jersey Div. at Dumps. Inspected H.Q. D.A.C. Van. Pack train out.	
	14		Sunny. Mr Schorpher M.S. cycle leaving for 6.15pm. 118 returns to	
			with B.H.Q. Wagon Line Cudr. at Tenure rd. agreed for 139 D = Arrival	
			M.Cork Arfeed. at K.B.R.A. at Tenure for more persons. 6.15pm a reinforcement	
	15		Cold rain, mountainous arrived. Section held up with Aust. from Bay Dump. Inspected	
Servins	16		Fair. 10 reinforcements arrived.	
	17		Cold windy rain travelled from Servins & St Catherine. Arranged with S.C 31st	
			& O.C. 2 D.A.C. stores. open 31st Dump. Capt Nathan & R.E. 2 H.D.W. Sgt Nolan	
			Km R.E. & 2 D.A.C. fairly gelling.	
	18		Fine & mild. Supply of Amn. by pack ways: motor and ub. wages Dump.	
St Catherine	19		Dull. 2 Div. gunners here. at H.Q. R.A. at Janas Dump	
	20		Mild rain. 1st Brigade 6 m saw reports from Rein. Bns J Brigade, D.A.C.O	
			3 C Stores 6 S Sent. 15 Tenth + 200 Shells from D.A.C.O	
	21		Fine mild. 20 men from D.A.C. 836. 139pr road fatigue, light raining from A.R.h.	
			6 Tank Dump. D.C.gun - S. Hale No 1 Sect R Ew. Shelton. Horse	
	22		Fair + clear. 11 Recuts + 13 Dr's 6 139 Du. reinforcements Capt Robin Sect 6.	
			Rest Camps. 108 Reinforcements Arrival from 50 pr Div H/4, 58 pr Oth. wicks, 13 clerks to DAC	

Vol II

WAR DIARY
or
INTELLIGENCE SUMMARY.
(Erase heading not required.)

Army Form C. 2118.

2nd D.A.C.

April 1917

Place	Date	Hour	Summary of Events and Information	Remarks and references to Appendices
St Catherine	23		Clear and warm. Very heavy firing. 6 Guns & 6 Sgts Guns from Base under 2/Lt Cape and No 1 R.A.	
	24		Fine + sunny. L/Cpl Clark g/N°3x" & 16 Bdy. 1 Hora Kelso No 2 x" L/Cpl Boreman li & Light Railway. Duty. Unposted Stone rails g/N° 2 + 3 x".	
	25		Clear. Warm. 8 Arrivals & 1st and Camps. Unposted N°1 x" Arrivals.	
	26		Main g.c.a.b. E.G.B. Works Dumps + R.A. H.A. Lgt Railway working late.	
	27		Fine. 8 Removals g/N° 2 x" killed shell fire.	
	28		Fine Rain. Suspected firings for New Dumps. Sam S.G.A. + 3.G.A RA Oc Samn. L. Grantope G. 13. Q. & G. 15 H.	
	29		Fine Warm. At New Dumps L/Bellew instructed+ discontinuing same. Wagon + Pack S/16/13 a work. New Dumps. Works Hq RA Bng (1) Clear. 11 B & 8 Pa send to Brigade, 2 recruits arrive. Lieu 1st arrival at New Dumps.	
	30		Red (Recruit). L/Cpl Gore took over New Dumps + L/Bellew 6.45 17513. Works Took over Dumps + Hq R.H.	

O.C. 2nd D.H.Q

2nd Divisional Artillery.

2nd DIVISIONAL AMMUNITION COLUMN R.F.A.

MAY 1917.

WAR DIARY or INTELLIGENCE SUMMARY

Army Form C. 2118.

Vol II

May 1917

2nd D.A.P.

Vol 34

Place	Date	Hour	Summary of Events and Information	Remarks and references to Appendices
St Catherine	1		Fine. Warm. Tivoli RA, RH, RUR, Dumps & No.1 X. Hands on Dumps & Rwy Bde Ras. G. 31st Div. recovering Amn. & Stores. Lgth Railway. General working on Supply.	
	2		Fine & Warm. Everything under Salving. Auxn Amzn Rd. 2 Eng & Coolies for Signal Stores & Wires & 27 OR Johnston Base Details Working parties. General Railway & Supply.	
	3		Fine. Very warm. Shells by Enemy during night 2 & 3 Enemy Planes over Tenneton. 3 Hrs on Horlim. Capt Malcolm reported from R.E. Railways exit O.O. This as transport L [...] T.M.s Personnel & Kent. General Railway Rwy R.S.	
	4		Fine. Fine. Enemy Aeroplane dropped 6 bombs in vicinity of Cmn. Several Horses of Wds Wounded. Visited HQ RA on horse & charge with O/cm arrangemts & closing of T.M.s No Wnd. 6 Eng Cas to Cmn. No Neville actg Adjt. Capt Malcolm returned to RE. Rest	
	5		Fine. Prisoner reported from Base at AFP Post count. Sergeant No 2 & 3 X". Lieutenant No 2 & 3 X"|. RA	
	6		Fine. 7 Guns & 12 DT 6 13 yd. reinforcements. 30 L.D. rein[forcem]ents from Base. Trails 179 RA Rosties etc.	
	7		Fine. Arranged [...] of work with Noov. & W ARP ([?]Control) General Routine etc	
	8		Fine. Clearing empties. Salving. General Routine etc.	
	9		Light Rain. Clearing empties. Salving.	
	10		Fine Clear. Salving. Clearing empties. 6 Bots joined from Base. Escorting overland at ARP HQs. Enlisted for Remounts 3 form Cmn. & hyn. ARP General	
	11		Fine. 2 Bots joined from Base. Clearing empty's. Salving, & hyn. ARP General Routine etc.	
	12		Fine. Salving. Clearing empties. General Routine etc.	
	13		Fine. Salving. Clearing empties. Work on ARP. General Routine etc.	
			Fine. Route RA HQ ARP. Clearing Empties. 5 O & 31 Guns & 7 Sig wallers. George & joined from Base. General Routine etc.	
	14		Rain. Strong night. 18 Guns 19 D & 7 Sig Cln 6 & 50 yds. 24 men & 3 N.C. from Tht 13th y. General & Routine etc.	

Army Form C. 2118.

WAR DIARY
or
INTELLIGENCE SUMMARY.
(Erase heading not required.)

Vol VI   2 New D.A.C.

May 1917

Place	Date May	Hour	Summary of Events and Information	Remarks and references to Appendices
Station	15		Fine + cool. 2/Lt P.S. Smith + Gough to 1st/1st Bty. 2/Lt Davis to 91st Bty. 2/Lt Gone to 71st Bty. 2/Lt Henderson to Gunnes. 4 Wagons to Dumps coy waterg. Visits Dumps + R.A.H.Q. General Routine etc.	
	16		Cloudy, rain. Army Officer. 2/Lt Huckley, 6.15 Bty. 4 Wagons to Dumps. 3 Mules. B.Am.S. Mules to Transfers. 6.28th B.A.C. 25 (B.S.M.) inspected H.Q. N°2 + N°3 X° Reserve combs etc 16 Dumps fatigue. General Rotational.	
	17		Cloudy. Heavy rain during night (16.17) 2/Lt Mead goes to 7 days leave. 4 Wagons to Dumps fatigue. General Rotational.	
	18		Clear + cool. 33 horses + 17 mules horses to 84th AFA Bgde. 4 Horses to Res'. Bgde 4 Wagons to Dumps fatigue. General Rotational. Visits Dumps + R.A.H.Q.	
	19		Fair. 4 Horses + 20 men away every gunner ammunition Bgde Major 1 Wagon to Barracks. Country Rd. No RA. 2 Wagons moving kits + Stores from 94 B.A.C. 6.5" Dr. to General etc. From 6 Gun AD to 6 Bgde's a Newfoundsts. Party to Boulogne leaves 33 Parcels for 36 Bgde. Cap't Wickham Deptd 4 days leave to Paris. Visits Dumps + R.A.H.Q. General Rotational etc.	
	20		Fine. 4 Wagons Dumps fatigue. 2/Lt Hughes agmt from Majors General Routine etc.	
	21		Rainy. 2/Lt Kirkton to 91st Bty. 2/Lt Buckner to 6 D/36 Bty. General Routine etc.	
	22		Fine, very warm. 2/Lt Johnson to 47th Bty. 2 mules, Horner Dram attached to 47 Kite Ry. Visits Dumps RAHQ. General fatigues etc. Arrival of H.Q. N°2 + 3 X° Kits for Pleurier.	
	23		Fine. 2/Lt Wickie 6.41st B.Bgde 2 NCOs 34 men to Boulogne Escort 70 recruits. Capt Boyd 6 Cow. S.A.A. arriving from Corbie. General Routine etc.	
	24			
	25			

Army Form C.2118.

WAR DIARY
or
INTELLIGENCE SUMMARY.
(Erase heading not required.)

Vol II
2nd D.A.C.
May 1917

Place	Date	Hour	Summary of Events and Information	Remarks and references to Appendices
St Etienne	26		Fine weather. Lt Colvin & O.C. proceeded to Caen. Lt Moore returned to Caen. Nos 2 & 3 X'd lorries came to Madagascar Camp. 21 mailbags arrived from Boulogne. Civil 33 renewals for No 361 B.Q.R. Capt Ranulty joins from Base in by mail. Lichied Kiw cupolas in Rolin & 7th Battn.	
	27		Fine Warm. 140 O.R's arrived to Madagascar Camp 21 Welsh from No 1 & No 3 & 50 duty. General Routine etc.	
	28		Fine Warm. 3 Horses have had camp greatly improved. 2 Bayons & Dumps Fatigue Cloudy. Lightrain. Visited Dumps & FA H.Q. Inspects No 2 & 3 Br. General Routine	
	29			
	30		Fine. Lightrain. Laique etc.	
	31		Fine. Cloudy in forenoon. Visited Dumps R.A.H.Q. Etc Same arrived from Boulogne with 230 renewals. Lt Pinkeley 613, & Lt 1076 both. General Roche in Hospital. Lt Cox joins from Hospital.	

AsDay L. Col
2nd D.A.C.

2nd Divisional Artillery.

2nd DIVISIONAL AMMUNITION COLUMN R.F.A.

JUNE 1917.

Army Form C. 2118.

WAR DIARY
or
INTELLIGENCE SUMMARY.

(Erase heading not required.)

Vol II
June 1917

2 Q.H.Q.
Vol 35

Place	Date	Hour	Summary of Events and Information	Remarks and references to Appendices
Kantara on Rly.	June 1		Fine. Rep'd Cols. Arbitrating between Personnel, office issues 31/5/17.	
	2		Wagon, 6 Dumps, Fatigues. General Routine etc.	
	3		Fine cloudy, visited Dumps. 6 Wagon & Dumps fatigues. 2/E.R.E. re Ro3S L. for fire hose. Inspected No. 1 X. General Routine, etc.	
	4		Fine clear. 1 Wagon + lcm. 5 O.R. 6 A.P.M. for Adj. R.E. + E.R.E. Service Lines in D.A.C. hire. Interview to C.M. at Q.M.Q. General Routine, etc.	
	5		Fine Warm. Dumps inspected by Cpn. 9.O.C. + E.R.E. inspects hoses.	
	6		2 + 3 x + 14 Q. 2 Wagon to T.M. for Adj. General Routine etc.	
	7		Fine. General Routine etc. Works Dumps. H.Q. R.E.	
	8		Fine. General Routine etc.	
	9		Fine tent showers Army afternoon. 20 Pers + 17 Sm inspected. Arrived from Ketan.	
	10		Fine very warm. L'e Busch + L'e Eire returned from Cairo. Inspd. hire Damps Phils. + H.Q. R.T.H. General Routine etc.	
			2 L'. Steu Flenury. 135 x + 13 fr aerofs and ets. Amir. hr. re. Payed.	
			General Routine etc.	
	11		Fine Very warm. 1/c. Starford + L'e Hughs 6 Eng Cas'r an Leave. General Routine etc. 10 Men L'e Peunes + 16 D. 2 hylicen 6 1590L rif Debn action. from Payed. General Routine etc.	
			G. M. 2/15/17. F. fatigue work. Cpn H.Q. Weeden Sheer gathering. Peunas Routine etc. 2 L' Palin 5 R.A. R.F.C. General Routin + 22 1/M Mysan. Debn. 2 N.Co. + 39 O.R. 6.	
	12		Fine L'e Nickin + June from T.M. course. No. 4 Permnnt Depot. for Personnel. General Routine + 2	

WAR DIARY or INTELLIGENCE SUMMARY

Army Form C. 2118.

2nd D.A.C.

Vol II June '17

Place	Date	Hour	Summary of Events and Information	Remarks and references to Appendices
Mazagon Barracks	1917 13		Fine. Visited Dumps & No.1 M.T. General Routine etc.	
	14		Fine. 4 men 6 T.M. came at 11:30am. Capt. O'Brien on leave. O/Lg. Sergt B.S.M. Kincaid Louisbourg 3" Howitzers. 6 No. D.A.C. B.S.M. Gosts 6. 17/3/17. B.S.M. Lewis op.pm 5 Louisbourg 3" Howitzers. 6 No. D.A.C. B.S.M. Gosts 6. 17/3/17. B.S.M. Lewis op.pm 5 D.A.C. General Routine etc.	
	15		Fine. "L" Howrs 6.36A B.30c (Reinfs) Inspected. No.2 & 3 Sub Rtne etc "L" Howrs 2L" Decon returns from Leave	
	16		Fine. Very warm. O.I.A. + D.D.V.S. inspected horses of D.A.C. General Routine etc.	
	17		Fine. Cloudy morn. 2L/o. 17.0 & 11 Reinforcements from Base (acknowledged) 3 Pers & Pr General Routine etc. Visited H.P.M.A.	
	18		6 T.M. newcomers General Routine etc.	
	19		Fine. Warm. L/o. Moyes & L/o. Deboo arrived from Base with 81 accounts Lorry attributed 119 6 units reinforcements from B'pore amongst 13000. D.A.C. Cloudy. Heavy thunder storm & rain. Others 3 horses. General Routine etc. 10. O.R. returned from Palestine at	
	20		Warm cloudy. G.O.C. of Army inspects Dumps General Routine etc	
	21		Cloudy. L/1 Hughes returns from Base Brigade. 2L Mackhern & Capt't Capt Cloudy. Rain during forenoon L/Cpl. Shaw leaves; wants to home via P. Canada. General Routine	
	22		Cloudy. L/Capt Lewis from 15th Batty Sergt Major 15:00 transfers to A.R.P. No 2 Cessn et Way on L.S. Cloudy. A.R.P. G.O.C. 13 Army inspects A.R.P. Verified his No.2 Guns etc 10 days Getting A.R.P. General Routine etc. D' had num 2 ft per long cord. 10 days	
	23		leave	

Army Form C. 2118

WAR DIARY
or
INTELLIGENCE SUMMARY.

2nd D.A.C.

Vol II
June 1917

(Erase heading not required.)

Instructions regarding War Diaries and Intelligence Summaries are contained in F. S. Regs., Part II. and the Staff Manual respectively. Title pages will be prepared in manuscript.

Place	Date	Hour	Summary of Events and Information	Remarks and references to Appendices
Madagascar Co	June 24		Gen. General Kantine etc.	
	25		Cloudy, visits H.Q.R.A. 2/13th Reports from Base attacked 2 x? O.H.C. General Kantine etc. Cloudy free from enemy.	
	26.		Cloudy, shiny N.W. wind. Fired K.Q.R.A. supports N° 2 & 3 x T General Kantine etc. Left cloud. 2" Stay 6 + 15" O.K from D.A.C - 9 O.K from 36" B gds. 6 Bon Coss	
	27.		filled up and fire in General Kantine etc. N° 2 & 3 Redan filled up and fire in for Reserve. General Kantine etc.	
	28		Heavy shower during E. & morning. General Kantine etc. P. Siedbourn 6 laylaid 10 days leave. 6 O.R. and 6.	
	29		Cloudy, shower forenoon. General Kantine etc. D.36 position fatigues. General Kantine etc.	
	30.		Rain during forenoon. General Kantine etc.	

[signature] Col.
Cmd 2 D.A.C

2nd Divisional Artillery.

2nd DIVISIONAL AMMUNITION COLUMN R.F.A.

JULY 1917.

WAR DIARY
or
INTELLIGENCE SUMMARY.

(Erase heading not required.)

Army Form C. 2118

2ⁿᵈ D.A.C.

Vol II

Vol 36

July 1917.

Place	Date	Hour	Summary of Events and Information	Remarks and references to Appendices
Madagascar X rd.	July 1		Cool, cloudy. R.K.Pct King cur Raids out. S.P. S.Wagon 6.36" Byde + 41st Bgde. 2 F.S.Wagon 6" N.A. X rd preparing for cars. Pencil Routine etc.	
	2		Clear & warm. Reliefs from Madagascar X ... & Bethune arrived/Bethune at 4 PM. 2 Ph Bur + Hy Ens 6.1st Army A.C. School HrE.	
Bethune	3		Fair, warm. 2/Lt Hughes from Bertangue with 66 Field. H.Q. 2 + 3 X" will Renard's wed to Pencilis. Copt Hoolje to Returned from low. General Routine etc.	
Pencilis	4		Fair, warm. took over from 66th D.A.C. 11 E.B.Wagon. 6 T.M. Bely.	
	5		Fine + warm. Dishechuli Renards. Strenuh 40, D.A.C. 26. Sankine Sec & Anne G.S.West General Routine etc. Capt Mellon retumed from leave.	
	6		Fine, cloudy. 2/Lt Henderson from leave. 2 Feton Joined from Base. 6 C.A.T. 6 205 K Cy. Labor Corps Curby 2ⁿᵈ Div R.O. 373. 6/7. At HQ R.A. Servir at Routine etc. Instructs issued for 2 + 3rd General Routine 6.36 Byde 18 inch Rawn's Heavy Thunderstorms during night. 22ⁿᵈ Janey + 6 F.A. bely sealed in from General Routine etc.) Unit Heavy Dust. +As Everard ... TM: L. Beurg Dump	
	7		Changed outlook. Col. 18th & S. Radion 6.6 Hykes Routine. Takymy 6 7Ph1 2° horse 2ⁿᵈ Hadensol fthorsh 6, Nort. 20 DR + 2 N.C.o. Gen R dalymy 6 7Ph1 2° horse 6 Lake Cul. No1 Yu Celrer 6 knel H.A.O 446. 6/7. Renered 500 f-7 13-X from 49th Div. General Routine etc.	
	8		Windy. 2ⁿᵈ Byd + 2ⁿᵈ Welsh Baws. 1 officer 10 OR 6 Bealize for Renards. General Routine etc.	
	9			
	10			

Army Form C. 2118.

WAR DIARY
or
INTELLIGENCE SUMMARY.
(Erase heading not required.)

Vol II   2nd D.A.C.
July 1917.

Place	Date	Hour	Summary of Events and Information	Remarks and references to Appendices
Vendeuil	11		Fine weather. Visits R.A.H.Q.	
	12		Fine weather. Visits Bouzy Dump. 12DT 6th Section Chalons Road Fatigues.	
	13		L. Grossman returned from leave. 8 day rest. General Routine &c. Light wind. Fine weather. L. Mortoban to No 2 x 22nd McKenna approved.	
			Hour 49. 16th Div. General Routine &c.	
	14		Dull. Thunderous evening. Entraining. L. Henderson returned from leave. Fatigue S.C. called. General Routine &c.	
			at Roche.	
	15		Cloudy. Showery Breeze. L. Sedgen & Scott arrived from Base. L. Sedgen 6.	
			No 1 Section L. Scott to 6-41st Bgde. L. Hughes arrived with 142 Renewals.	
			from Boulogne. L. McKenna to No 1 Section. L. Boyd 6 No 3 L.	
			L. Wolsey 6 - No 2 7 ". Visits H.Q. R.A. 22 Renewals from	
			Box Cage for 2nd Div. A.R. arrived at No 1 Section. S.C. R.A. wispec.	
			General Routine &c.	
	16		Fair. Distribution 142 Renewals (36th Bgde 5-8 41st Bgde 26 D.A.C 58.-)	
			Establishment of Ammn Ch. Guns increased 6 R. St. 300 per gun 18 P.	
			Cartr Rifle 500 pr R. 18P. 250 rd Rd Gun 4.5 How.	

WAR DIARY
or
INTELLIGENCE SUMMARY.
(Erase heading not required.)

Vol II 2nd D.A.C.

July 1917

Army Form C. 2118.

Place	Date	Hour	Summary of Events and Information	Remarks and references to Appendices
Headqtrs (B) Béthune	17		Lieut. Seary & Cpl. L. Cpl. Dayeh proceed to 10 days leave. Also 4 O.R. detm on 30 days leave. 2 P.Pts Rein from leave. Capt. R. Pd leave arrived evd. S.O.R. General Routine etc.	General Routine
	18		How our avg D. Wrigly rengy. Col. Villar Stewart visits. Lines B.P.O.	General Routine
	19		"Hughes" & A.P.P. Heavy rain during recovery. General Routine etc.	
	20		Line relief. 5 O.R. return from T.M. Course. D.D.R. visits. Evg of Nº 1 X² cadets 2 hours. 4 N.C.O.'s & 8 O.R. School of Cookery Béthune. A.D.V.S inspects H.Q. Horses. General Routine etc.	S.A.A.x
	21		Lieut Everard S.O.E. R.A. 11th Corps visits D.A.C lines. 4 S.O.R. Officers + 12 men for S.A.A.x and S.O.E R.A. 11th Corps left for Bridge for armourers. A.R.P. to Chocques General etc.	General Routine etc.
	22		20 Wrights & 36th Bdge Reinf W charge. General Routine etc. 2 P. W.O.R. Reinf W charge. General Routine etc.	
	23		Lieut Brig W.O. visits New Line Nº 4 + 2 + 3 D.A.P. General Routine etc. S.A.Q.F. 5.9gr 25 lb. 6.4½ 130gr + 2gr 6.36x 15dja co reinforcements. N. 2X² ammd 6 lb charge. N.O 3X² ammd W.8d 354. Cpl. Weston agon loan from N. 2X² ammd 6 lb Charge. N.O 3X² attached N.O 3X². General Routine etc.	
	24		Sick leave. S.S.F.S. Heacock joined from Base. 2 N.C.O.'s & 12 Lieut Warren. Cpl Boston. Errk on dry. A.R.P & Choquege P.S. General Routine etc.	
	25		School lessons for 2 days Course. General Routine etc. C. St Hernet. D.A.C Races. Many Shand visitors arrived. S.O.R & every dsen Béthune X² on agon Standings de Nos Cuivo. General Routine etc.	

WAR DIARY or INTELLIGENCE SUMMARY.

Army Form C. 2118.

(Erase heading not required.)

Vol II   2 D.A.C.   July 1917.

Place	Date	Hour	Summary of Events and Information	Remarks and references to Appendices
Béhune	26		Bde G. warn. Con. Nr. for relative of horses for Bording Parties. Wrote D.A.C.	Raining
	27		2/Lt. Sigden joined & returned from Boulogne with 69 Remounts. Raining & cool. 3 Officers 2 D.A.C. attended attend. by Col. Bob & Vest. 2/Lt. Hogg & penns a on Course Es G. a S. 1, 2 & 3 in absence of Cmn. General Ruthven.	Raining Rec lie et. General Rec lie et. General Ruthven et.
	28		Bins & Corn. 2/Lt. Henderson from T.M. Burg.	General Ruthven.
	29		Much down 2/Lt. Crick 5/Lt. Shepard from 1st A.A. School.	General Ruthven.
	30		Raining. 2 N.Co's to Lesca gas school for 4 days Burg. 2 S.S.9. 1 Bdys & compant. 16 cdl. 2/L. Newson & 1/2 T.M.B. A.D.V.S. visits Ame lui. 1/Lt. Daly L.st from 10 days leave. 1/Lt. Sherman from Base fools & 1/L 2.	General Rutlandt.
	31		Cwit & relax. NCO's N:IX; Dunfos. N:2 + 3"; Crin; obtain & same during Cuins. also APP in used for same; Bde's HQRA General Rutheroti. 1/Lt. Sherman to 15 th 13th. 1/Pearson 6 - 2 - 2 T.M. B.H.	

Maclyn h f Ge 2 D A C

2nd Divisional Artillery.

2nd DIVISIONAL AMMUNITION COLUMN R.F.A.

AUGUST 1917.

Army Form C. 2118.

WAR DIARY
or
INTELLIGENCE SUMMARY.
(Erase heading not required.)

Vol II
August 1917
2nd D.A.C.

Place	Date	Hour	Summary of Events and Information	Remarks and references to Appendices
Béthune	1		Heavy Rain. Sergt "Whit." Sergt "White" No 1 X 6.71 of 13th. A.R.O.N.G. 2nd Div. North No 3 X' Guns. Pt Boyd to Hospital. Sergt Holland + Pt Horn. 1 Offr. Bohun. 6 trains on 13th filled. General Routine etc.	
	2		Raining. 12 [?] from Base as reinforcements. General Routine etc.	
	3		Rainy + close. L' Thornce + Stopford arrived on leave from Aus. 1st Mt units around Arlin a Coy. General Routine etc.	
	4		Mild + Light Rain. L' Pevenne - 17 OR + Boulogne to reinforcements. General Routine etc.	
	5		Mild + close. 2 NCOs + 900 Cause Leave 4 days. 10 offrs 2 NCOs 508 to special parade Army War.	
	6		Section working at Plodsius + Quin. General Routine etc. Mild + thick. 1 Sergt 2 SS went [?] from Base. Thick. No 1 X A.K.P. General Routine etc.	
	7		Overcast + dull. Aspinwar elm + Sergt Q. 13 leave. Rectif from D.A.C. for reports of 2 Batalls. General Routine etc.	
	8		Thick. Visits N° 2 X Guns. General Routine etc. Fine + mild. 2 L' Jessop span b arrived from Base with reinforcements (32). Bovis despatch Q. E.A. Ply U army. 6 H.D. B.A.P. General Routine etc.	
	9		Fine + close. 22 R'rept to reinforce from base. Visits A.T.P. N°3 X Guns. R.A.H.Q. 32 Reinforcements. Air attacks as follows: 36 + 13 gds 12. D.A.C 16. Pay gds. Guide 4. General Routine etc.	
	10		Mild + clear. Sergts E.L.A 2/L Leave + L.L. Edy Capt. + General N°1 X. Capts to L'ance forward to Town. L' Goodg. from N°2 G N°3 X. N° 35718 Pr W.E. Edwards whilst on fatigue at 7th 13th. General Routine etc.	

Army Form C. 2118.

Instructions regarding War Diaries and Intelligence Summaries are contained in F. S. Regs., Part II. and the Staff Manual respectively. Title pages will be prepared in manuscript.

Vol II

WAR DIARY
or
INTELLIGENCE SUMMARY.

2. D.A.C.

19. August 1917.
(Erase heading not required.)

Place	Date	Hour	Summary of Events and Information	Remarks and references to Appendices
Bethune	Aug. 11		Mild robin shower in afternoon. 2nd Lt. McKenna attached to 2 T.M.O. 13th Bty.	
	12		2 Lt. Sutton from No 3 & No 1 X" 15 OR returns from Fatigues at T.M.O. 13th. Battn. General Paragon visits No 2 X" TMHQ.	
	13		Fine Warm. 15 OR 6 Div Sigs School passed using 6 The Course Commencing at Cloysus on the 14 inst. Sergt R.A. & Day separated from 3rd Div. General Routine etc. visits.- Heavy Thunderstorms.	
	14		Fine & Clear. 3 Gun exchanged with ? from D.31"B.M. (and Age) visits RAPD visits N°3 X". General Routine etc.	15/8/24
	15		Fine Clear. Heavy rain during Evening. 2/Lt Kruger & 4 OR 64th Brigade at Cherence. Capt. McRae RAMC received on leave. Parton began leads on 6. 47. 13th. 2/Lt Bennett. 2/Lt Bennett & D 36. 13th. From 13th Bde Pools to N°3 X". General Routine etc.	
	16		Wild Clear. Lts Hinde & 2/Lt Shepherd returned from leave. Lts H.B. HA N° 2 X". A.R.P. General Routine etc. Lts visits N°3 X". General Routine etc.	
	17		Fine Sunny. Interview with D.A.D.V.S. Heavy shells burn 6 Bns on Bethune. 2/ 2 Wobs from N°3	
	18		Fine & Clear. 2/Lt Debroy from leave. 2 Wobs from M.U.S. taken to steamy Tr. General Routine etc. 2/ N° 2 X" visits N° 2 X" Visits M° 2 X" RDKA General Routine etc.	
	19		2/ N° 2 X" visited. General Routine Visits N° 3 X" A.R.P. and delivered of N° 3 X" at Vaudin. Brig W. Farm	19 L"
	20		Fine & Sunny. 2/Lt Wholly & 2/Lt McYere & Camouflage Comm. Wimereux. D Horse & Posse 16.8 for interview with Van & coating the invented General Routine	

Army Form C. 2118.

WAR DIARY
or
INTELLIGENCE SUMMARY.
(Erase heading not required.)

2nd D.A.C.

Vol II

August 1917

Instructions regarding War Diaries and Intelligence Summaries are contained in F.S. Regs. Part II. and the Staff Manual respectively. Title pages will be prepared in manuscript.

Place	Date	Hour	Summary of Events and Information	Remarks and references to Appendices
Béthune	Aug 21		Fine & clear. Inspected HQ 2nd DAC. Proceeded on 5 days Special leave 8 Aug 21. C.O.	
	22		Fine & clear. Capt. Wood handed over to No22 Vet. Hospital Abbeville. Capt. McKeon administers Baux. Capt. Dunlop A.V.C. took over duties from Capt. Wood. General Routine.	
	23		Fine & clear. Showers during evening. 1 Gunner transferred to D3C. Capt. McKeon O/c "3X". Assumed duties of C.O. DAC. General Routine &c.	
	24		Fine & cool during morning. Showery during afternoon. 2/Lt Woods & 2/Lt Mc Venzie O/c guards from Camouflage Corps. General Routine &c.	
	25		Fine & clear. General Routine &c.	
	26		Fine & clear. Heavy rain during night. 2/Lt McIlroy & 4 N.C.O. returned from Tp & Bomb School. 15 men & 2 teams from T.M. Battery. 2/Lt Woolman & 2/Lt Evans posted to 1st Army H.A. asst. Corps. Lt. Col Delafield returned from leave. General Routine etc.	
	27		Fine & clear. Raining during afternoon. 2/Lt Logsdon 25 O.R. proceeded to the Army 1st Army School of Instruction. Cm. 10 OR. S.D.C leave. N° 2 X° General Routine &	
	28		Stormy. Heavy rain. General Routine.	
	29		Stormy. Again. 55 reinforcements from Bartays. Trials N° 3 X". Gen. P. General Routine etc.	
	30		Wind Veering. Rain during afternoon. DA.S.U.S. inspects Remts. Name &h details as follows. 36th Bde. 24, 41st Bde. 22. Duty units 9. General Routine &h.	
	31		Nice Showery. Detachment N° 3 X" Open Carso & Lee. Clay arms. Capt. McKeon parade. Ccm. 10 D. O.R. T.C.F.A & reinforcements from Base. General Routine &c.	
			Gen. Clyde 8/G/l, L. Col Cmd'g 2nd DAC	

2nd Divisional Artillery.

2nd DIVISIONAL AMMUNITION COLUMN R.F.A.

SEPTEMBER 1917.

Army Form C. 2118.

WAR DIARY
or
INTELLIGENCE SUMMARY.
(Erase heading not required.)

Vol II 2nd D.A.H.Q. September 1917 Vol 38

Place	Date	Hour	Summary of Events and Information	Remarks and references to Appendices
Bethune	Sept. 1		Visits other. Visits HQRA N°3X°. A.R.P. N°1X°. General Rankin etc.	
	2		Fine clear. 5-9pr 5.B°. 6.36"15½c. 5.B°. 6-4½".Byde. 2.B° 6.T. Trans. General Rankin	
	3		Fine clear. Warm. Enemy shelling Vendin. Visits RAHQ N°3X° A.R.P. N°2X° General Rankin -	
	4		Fine clear. Capt Malkin posted to Army School Maysui. Visits HQ DAC etc. General Rankin etc.	
	5		Fine warm. Visits N°2X°. A.R.P. N°3X°. General Rankin etc.	
	6		Fine & Clear. Enemy Gun enft. engaged bomb way HQRAC tying to camp 6 mm to ammk.	
			D.A.C. X° Cross Rover. Visits HQ. D.A.C. Lines. General	
			& Cook Howes inspected. 29 Div. Reinfs. arrived from Base.	
			Rankin etc.	
	7		Cloudy. Visits N°2X° Lines. A.R.P. N°3X° Lines. General Rankin etc.	
	8		Dull. Visits N°3X° Lines A.H.Q. 25 Gunners Reinforcements from Base. General Rankin etc.	
	9		Clear. 1 N.C.O. + 2 O.R. 6: 1st Army A.H.Q. 1 Lt CH Weston on leave England. (Wakely)	
	10		Mosly. 3 D° & 6 Gun. 6-36" Byde. 1 O.R. & V.S.T.M. 1 O.R. & Western 6- A.R.P. Visits 2 + 3 X° DAC General etc.	
			100R on ARP. Visits DAC A.R.P. visit SC etc.	
	11		Fine Bright. 15 O.R. B-TM. Course. 1 Pro. Enemy School. 10 OR A Marks T.M. 10 OR 6 A.R.P. & Post	
			6. RE Officers. 2 L. Padger + 25 O.R. returned from T.M. Course. 2nd Lieut. returned 6 N°2X°	
	12		Fine Bright. 2 L. Snyder Posts. 6. Y. 2 T.M. 151 4. 2 OR refresponsible. To V.S.T.M. Bly.	
	13		Windy. Visits SAA. N°2 + 3 X°. 5 O.R. from 45 T.M. 14 & takes over. General Cambun etc.	
	14		Nice. Mosly. 1 Sgt 1 B.T. Sub exam. Posted for 71.4.15 14. 29 OR joined from Base. General Rankin etc.	
	15		Fine clear. 1 B° 10 OR 6 36" Bdgs. 1 B° 6-4.10" Bgdc. General Rankin etc.	

A 5834 Wt. W4973 M687 750,000 8/16 D. D. & L. Ltd. Forms/C.2118/13.

WAR DIARY or INTELLIGENCE SUMMARY

Army Form C. 2118.

Vol II 2nd D.A.C.
Title pages September 1917.

Place	Date	Hour	Summary of Events and Information	Remarks and references to Appendices
Battery	16	Fine clear	1° HC Weston returns from leave. Gen'l Rankin etc.	
	17	Fine clear	A.D.O.S XI Corps inspects HQ D.A.C. Gen'l Rankin etc.	
	18	Fine rain	visits RA NQ. No.2 & Brosey Dumps. Gen'l Turnbull	
	19	Fine clear	visits No.3 X". A.P.P. Gen'l Rankin etc.	
	20	Windy	visits S.A.A X". Gen'l Rankin etc.	
	21	Fine clear	Gen'l Rankin etc. Empress Indian R.D. Gen'l Rankin etc	
	22	Fine clear	15 CR guns from N°3 Reinforcement Camp. Gen'l Rankin etc	
	23	Fine clear	2 Majors in Spur Line. 9.0R 6.36" 5.0TT 6.4 13.9Dz. Reinforce	
			Southern in every class. D.AC collects 2 S.A.A X" escorting own	
	24	Fine rain	visits S.A.A X". Gen'l Rank etc.	
	25	Fine clear	150R from The Coune. 1M Car.18 P.P. Dayman. 3 F nurses 19.QT 6	
		Showers	Detact. Capt SFRgh. joins NQ D.T.C. Gen'l Rankin etc.	
	26	Fine clear	20 nurses xchang out 17.40 hrs pr L.D Horn Gen'l Rankin etc.	
	27	Misty Clear	visit SAA X" and A.D.V. inspects Supply Dumps. Gen'l Rankin	
	28	Fine clear	16R 6- N°7 NQ S.sup for Horsey 2 Pdr. 1 Sadr. 2 Joins from 15 Bdg	
	29	Fine clear	5.9CD air kitchels 6- 36+41 or 13Dz. visits N°2+3 X" 7HQ.P Brit Rabin etc	
	30	Fine clear	13" Donaldson 6- 11 Cpo NQ avery 36 405 21.9.17 Quil Rankin	

Geo A. Young Maj RA 2nd DAC

2nd Divisional Artillery.

2nd DIVISIONAL AMMUNITION COLUMN R.F.A.

OCTOBER 1917.

WAR DIARY or INTELLIGENCE SUMMARY

Army Form C. 2118.

Vol II 2nd D.A.C.

October 1917.

Place	Date	Hour	Summary of Events and Information	Remarks and references to Appendices
Bethune	Oct 1st		Line relief. 2 D.C. b. 36th Bde. 20 Reinforcements. General Routine etc.	
	2		Fine, 1st Relay. 12 OR. 2 NCO. attached to 7th Bde. Winches H.Q. R.H. 2+3 x reinforcements. General Routine etc.	Carried out 11 P.M.
	3		Cloudy & dull. 7 OR. 6 7th Bde 15th Bde. Fatigue. 38 NCO men OR's leave & detail on reorganisation of D.A.C. proceeded to R.A. Base Depot. G.O.C. Div. C.R.H. Inspected all sections of D.H.Q. General Routine etc.	
	4		Mild. rain during evening. General Routine etc.	
	5		Fine relief. 1 OR. Junior D.A.C. from base. Inspected foulances on 10 days leave England. Capt Stothgath proceeded 6-7½-10th.15th.17. 10 mules (Pumpers) 6 No F.A.B.Y.	2/Lt Major 6. returning from Sharpual Jones U.S. Army. General Routine etc.
	6		Mild. Windy. Sergt. Savage Tpt Dr 6-25th Div. P.R.D. +1 Mule issued to England. Trick's Dumps at Bovary. A.R.P. + S.A.A. Xt General Routine etc.	6 No F.A.B.Y. (Pumpers) 21. Gun Ammn (Reserve) es on 10 Major Line 6.
	7		Raw, rainy, cold. 2 Syn alm Junior from Base. General Routine etc.	Tricks No.2+3 x 4 H.A.D.+2 Lime.
NEDON	8		Cold. Rainy during day. D.A.C. moved from Bethune to NEDON. 6 Dunn...	
	9		6 Bgde. Reinforcements. Arriv. NEDON 2.15 P.M. General Routine etc.	
	10		Fine cloudy. Settling in new lines etc. Raining. 2 Signaler 6. 41st Bdge. Spel Purch attached E.T.Major Murray	R.H. Reinforcements of the Queens

Army Form C. 2118.

WAR DIARY
or
INTELLIGENCE SUMMARY.

Vol II 2"D.A.C.
October 1917

(Erase heading not required.)

Instructions regarding War Diaries and Intelligence Summaries are contained in F. S. Regs., Part II. and the Staff Manual respectively. Title pages will be prepared in manuscript.

Place	Date	Hour	Summary of Events and Information	Remarks and references to Appendices
NEDON	11		Fine. 6 L.D. & 9 wks march to N°3 M.V.S. Capt Weston 1 N.C.O & 2 drivers left on fats. Another. General Routine etc. visits Lieut 1, 2 & S.A.A. C.R.H visits Divn.	
	12		Col & Rainy Serj Vernon A.V.C. & R.Q 2 D.W. from D.A.C. General Routine etc A.D.V.S Benfield, Arrival of S.A.A Col 1.R.D	
	13		Rain in evening. Rain clear afternoon. 1 Serj 1, S.S, 17 OR proceeded to S.A.A Base. General Routine etc.	
	14		Fine colder. attended A.D.V.P necessary Examined. General Routine etc.	
	15		Misty. Clear. Rain heavy afternoon. Visits all X'mas lines. General Routine etc.	
	16		Fine. 5 G.S. Wagon & 36 & W sent. General Routine etc.	
	17		Fine. Clear. Lft McDon for Pleinbergia. Serj from R.W.C from N°2 X" & N°10 Vet Hospital. Serj & Keenan from N°2 Vet. Hospital to N°2 X" avail Reinforce 4 P.M	
Steenbeque	18		Divn. marches from Steenbeque to Pleinwoorde. Divnl Rendorde 3 P.M.	
Pleinwoorde	19		March from Steenbeque to Reige Camp Capt Weston with our Sorel Dumps Gork B Snan provides tea & Lug Eng S.	
Vlamwtugh	20		Clear. Sorrow train from 8"D.A.C. H.U.C Strid 2 8 N.W Boyrs. (Capt Wook/ n/k pet-ren) Mae Ears Cray L & S. G.S Wagon. 6 Sorrow Malso R.E Wyen. General Routine etc, Sec los Lines. Giese & Murphy James from tree. Luries anned with Amm t mob. Smbed. C.R.A inspects luies. Visit. H.A.R.D goltw. G.S Wagon N°1 X" Keetings G. Emor, Shelfirs.	
	21		General Routine etc.	

WAR DIARY or INTELLIGENCE SUMMARY

Army Form C. 2118.

Vol III
October 1917.

Place	Date	Hour	Summary of Events and Information	Remarks and references to Appendices
Wavrechain	22nd		Clear & fine. Visits X° Divnl. General Routine etc. Enemy's establishment of forward dumps at C.17.d.	C.17.d. 1-3.
	23		BD Patl. 16 guns 2 hrs. 6° Bgde. on reinforcements. 18 M.G.'s in new attacks. General Routine etc. B.S. Wagon No 2 X° Salvage by enemy shell fire.	D.A.A.P/man
	24		Fine. Clear. Shing & wind. General Routine etc. 5 enemy planes over camp 12 Noon.	
	25		Fine. Shing & wind. 7 G. 6.47 C. on reinforcements. 2.33 pm. 9 air from base 10 hour enemy's bivouac. General Routine etc.	
	26		Rain & wind. Capt. Dockson pressed in 10 days then suprised. Heavy shelling & bombing by enemy. 1 count of Corps. 3 animals wounded. General Routine etc.	
	27		Fine. Relief. 1 wounded sent to ambs. 6 M.U.S. visits X° General Routine etc.	
	28		Cos. Clear. Sg. Shotwell + 2 O.R. 6° N° 1 Gen. Workshps. Captten. General Routine etc.	
	29		Fine Clear. 16 G.o + 3 O.R. 6. B 9 b.c. on reinforcements. 1 horse killed 5 wounded. 2 O.R. wounds - by shell fire. Enemy Bn's. outposts. G° Bedford Casualty amb'ce. at Buch. General Routine etc.	
	30		Cos. Shing & wind. Rain during afternoon. 4 O.R. wounds. 6 L.D. Evac'd. y'day. N°1 X°. 4 L.D. Wounds. 4 & Wounds y'day. Shell fire. Am. Supply. Au L.S.Y.P.S.	3 L.D. Kills
	31		6. 3rd Can. Is. M.U.S. General Routine etc. 1 L.D. N°2 X°. killed. Shell fire. 2 L.D. + 2 Mus. Fine 9 G. 2 O.R. 6 3 6" 15 y.S. 24 G. 10 O.R. B 41 o. reinforcements. 2 L.D. Evac'd y'day 30 + enemy G° O'Bain attacks from here. General Routine etc.	2 O.A.Q.

Greatly est. I/6/2. 2 O.A.Q.

2nd Divisional Artillery

2nd DIVISIONAL AMMUNITION COLUMN R.F. A.

NOVEMBER 1917.

WAR DIARY or INTELLIGENCE SUMMARY

Army Form C. 2118.

November 1917 2nd D.A.C.

Place	Date	Hour	Summary of Events and Information	Remarks and references to Appendices
Marlborough	Nov. 1		Fine & clear. General Routine etc. Work'd train 1 & 2 X'ns	
	2	Midy	3 O.R. joined from Base. 1 mule & 1 x° died of wounds. 2 mules & 1 L.D. wasters etc. G.M.V.S. Wounds. General Routine etc.	
	3	Midy	B.Q.M.S. Payne from 282 Coy Bde Trn. 6 N°2 X'n. General Routine etc.	
	4	Midy	General Routine etc.	
	5		Fine & clear. General Routine etc.	
	6	Midy	Showery. 5 O.R. (S.o. 13.9) 6 36 th & 41st Bde. N°108561 R. Sutton killed & 5th Bde 5 L.D. Wounded by shell fire. N°2 X'n. 3 O.R. from Base as reinforcements. 30 Tn Men attached for duty. 3 O.R. from Base as reinforcements. General Routine etc.	
	7		1 L.D. casualty wounded. N°2 X'n. 1 aero king W. for wounds. General Routine etc.	
	8	C.o.W. running	1st Wagon. attacks 6 H.Q.R.A. work hard until 2 am. General Routine etc.	
		C.o. Showery.	Op'l train retired from line to Engh. General Routine etc.	
	9	Mid'y & Even	1 L.D. Cor'l from 41st Bgde (attache from D.H.Q.) George & France Pass Killed by Enemy Shell fire. General Routine. Wounded 2 mules killed 2 mules & 3 L.D. wounded 3. Enemy shell fire.	
	10	C.o. Rainy Weather	N°s 1 & 2 X'n. S.A.B. General Routine etc.	
	11	C.o. Raining	B.Q.M°r Farrow, D° Fairhurst Mud Corp & A. Brennan. Reported. St Catherine Wounds.	
		1 Kurd killed. Enemy Shell fire. General Routine etc.		
	12	Mid.y	3 O.R. 6 36 th Bgde. 2 L.D. casualties 6 M.V.S. L. Stock Ave. 648" B.14. L' Cope. from Tn. X'2 B.14. 6 SAAX. General Routine etc.	
	13		Fair. relief of Debris period W on 14 days leave to-day. Cas. N°22236 Gr Balkers Dennis evacuated hospit. General Routine etc.	
	14	Midy & Murky	15 th Redworth 6 15 L' B.14, evacuated. General Routine etc.	

Army Form C. 2118.

WAR DIARY
or
INTELLIGENCE SUMMARY.
(Erase heading not required.)

Vol II   2 D.A.C.

November 1917

Place	Date Nov.	Hour	Summary of Events and Information	Remarks and references to Appendices
Mauberge	15		Fine clear. General Routine etc.	
	16		Nich. Showers. 82 P.D. Germiston Base, 5" Kapley Horge & feeler covers & plate for " y wd. 1 Cell. 1 S.P. Wagn Rly. g.s hub no. General Routine etc.	
	17		Mich. General Routine etc.	
	18		Mich. General Routine etc. returned to Arnoe from Dumps. A 868 AX 792 Rds.	
			Mich. 990.000 S.A.A. returned to Corps Dump.	
	19		Clear Mist. 36 grs + 13 Dr. to 1 Bgd as reinforcements. All attached T.M. personnel returned	
			to Bn. 15 Cdn. Handed over 5.1 Dr. 266.18 Pdr + 126.4.5" Gun. 1" wds by + 50 BR	
			13 Dr. Pools to D.A.C. from 2nd D.T.M.S. Capt Offpen C.A.P. joined from 36" 130pc. 1 Sgl 3 Dr. 3.3 grs v	
			to base for remounts. General Routine etc.	
	20		Clear. Handed over lines 5.1 DW. Marched to Walsin.	
			Rain + Cold. 115" + 10 Sig walkers joined from Base. Pools & Horses arrive well.	
Walsin	21		177 remounts from Base. 2 O/Dig Lakeum. Ship by Jones from T & I Gen	
			Routine etc. Handed over 6.1 Dw. 4.5" + S.A.A. + Rds	
	22		6 wd bn g.10 Sig walkers 5.13 Dgs. Motor cycle and 'Collect. 18 Pr. 4.5' + S.A.A. + Rds	
			+ 35 L.D. drawn 1" Cornvid + Div Jones from Base Opi "Cornd" reeds. G.S.A. XX	
	23		General Routine etc.	
			Visid order. 1" McKenna ordered a Medical Board & which Isthmay E of D.T.Q.	
			1" Ship by perds. G.D.36.15.14. General Routine etc.	
	24		Cold Sleety Wind. 1 Go Pals 60 T.P.O. from V.27.M.S. returned D.T.A.O. at General Route +	
			Dopudbag. Cor. Allenwound Repping	

WAR DIARY or INTELLIGENCE SUMMARY

Army Form C. 2118.

Vol. II   2" D.H.C.

(Erase heading not required.)

November 1917.

Place	Date	Hour	Summary of Events and Information	Remarks and references to Appendices
Haplincourt	25		Mild clear. Arrived from Moramont. Poring during night of 24-25th. D'Gri 90. Horses grey & railway killed by a horse. D'Stanlis to Hospital from Lyndeburgh to Moramont. Lis air Ferme Rouhin etc. Mild clear. General Kouhin Jo.	Gnn en route.
	26			
Nurgnement	27		Cld. raining. March Pri Stoflereent. E Royaul Cnt. 600 NCO's & OR G HK.P. Fabijin established hun etc.	
	28		Mild; 37 Tents from 108 Bgde & deand G. 41st. 8. G.S. Wagons completed. Horse D'amis L'Gaine stocks G. M.A. Coy. Relief's proceed with for Stamp at K.15.6. General Kouhin etc.	
	29		Mild clear. Estab Welsh & Co HR G K.15.6 estab. hui. Dump. T.M.S.C. Nerunce Dump & acmis 36 Div T.M: General Kouhin etc.	
	30		Mild mild. P. Delos aimed from Cairo & Reg End. 2nd DTP. Cow air from 36 "DHC Ope. Offis & N°3 NG. Hospital. Sgt Phili Opl. Gab: D'Sweett, 9 Cllj Cowlis & Hospital. Connced by Shee hui. General Kouhin etc.	

Ashby hurst
C. R. E.

2nd Divisional Artillery.

2nd DIVISIONAL AMMUNITION COLUMN R.F.A.

DECEMBER 1917.

Army Form C. 2118.

Vol II   2 D.A.C.
Dec 1917

WAR DIARY
or
INTELLIGENCE SUMMARY.
(Erase heading not required.)

Instructions regarding War Diaries and Intelligence Summaries are contained in F.S. Regs. Part II. and the Staff Manual respectively. Title pages will be prepared in manuscript.

Place	Date	Hour	Summary of Events and Information	Remarks and references to Appendices
Bapaume	12.17			
	1		Misc. Misty. Capt. Ibrahim visits re Pierrrie Dumps. General Routine etc.	
	2		Clear. R.O.S. Pierrrie Dump to be closed down. Dumps at R.I.S. 6 closes.	
	3		L.t 2.0.R. going from Base.	
	4		Frost. Clear. R.e. Croti spring & Baker Junction from Base. General Routine etc.	
	5		Frost. Clear. 6.D. 5.G.S. saddle. 6.15.D.C. R.e. Walker Lawton Wood & Hartley joins 19ed. 25 D.C. 20 reinforcements from Base.	
	6		Frost. Heavy. Capt. McKern proceeds to England on 14 days leave. C.M. on Go Brennan. Adjourned. Cpl. Walker lives W.R. A.T.P.T. 36 R.D.V. Personnel returns 6: 2 O.T.M.3 General Routine etc.	
	7		Frost Heavy. 1.F.D. (reed) 2 L.D. Wounds. Whilst crossing Dne. from Arras and Peronne.	N° 547315, 120953. D° Bowden & Gordon
	8		W.47 4. 18.17 6. Pontoon occupied. General Routine etc. Misc. Clear. 1 B.Q.M.S. 1 Sgt. & 32 O.R. joins from Base.	
	9		Misc. Misty. Appt. Dumps closed. Packing equipments for reserve. Visits X.O. General Routine etc.	
	10		Rain. 2/Lt. Murray, 1 B.Q.M.S. 1.7.Sgt. joins from Base. General Routine etc.	
	11		Misc. very windy. R.A. Marshall Lawton Wood, Metcalf Walker attacks 636 R.D.V. N° 73891 D° Hughes admits to Hosp. wounds. General Routine etc. Lieut. Col. Renew T.M. Rounds at A.F.P. by Powell of D.A.P. Visits A.F.P. & X° General Routine etc.	

Army Form C. 2118.

WAR DIARY
or
INTELLIGENCE SUMMARY.

(Erase heading not required.)

Vol 2
2nd Div. Am. Col.
Dec. 1917

Place	Date	Hour	Summary of Events and Information	Remarks and references to Appendices
Mazar Gerid	12		Chief of Staff, Brig Gen Murry Q Brister, Col Inspector Qf Gof Q Depots, Packs etc/Picks	
			Near Rail line & reports ready for advance. General Routine etc.	
	13		Maj G. Visits HKP at Sand toggar. General Routine etc.	(General Routine etc.)
	14		Lt G. raw. Convoy. 2 L. Batt. proceeds for duty at Depot Depot. 2 New Guns returned ARR.	
	15		Brig H. Clerr. Visits HQRA. General Routine etc.	
Shepheards	16		Niss. Clerr. HQ. RAH × " moved to Hope in Cam. 1 × 2 × × 6. Boncourt erecting Lines etc"	
	17		Heavy fall snow. Visits HQRA. Capel Houses on base Stayed. Col H&Ag MC. Adj. B/K.	
			General Routine etc.	
	18		Indy. Cols. 3"D". 2.5" Guns joined from Base. Visits X". General Routine etc.	
	19		Maj G. General Routine etc.	
	20		Chief R Clo. 13 Lewis bodies Field Material for erection by 93rd BD/SC & DT/G. General Routine	
	21		Ford. 1 So. 3 Dr. joined from Base. 39L.D. Hows 17 Hunks arrived from Base. Move Stable	
			Material arriving. Enemy Shells. General Routine etc.	
	22		Units & Clerr. Reinforcement Battalions. Enemy Shell. General Routine etc.	
	23		Col W. Clerr. Enemy A. Craft Bomber. 1 × 2 × " 8 Carnochis including 2 Kicks	
	24		Cos. Wendy 40 Men from 30" Labr. B, assisting erection of Stables. General Routine etc.	

Vol II 2nd Div A.C.

Army Form C. 2118.

WAR DIARY
or
INTELLIGENCE SUMMARY.
(Erase heading not required.)

Dec 1917

Place	Date Dec	Hour	Summary of Events and Information	Remarks and references to Appendices
Achicourt	25		Mild slight haze. No 8847 G.O.P.W. Bailey found dead. Medical Officer.	Brokin it General A
	26		Heavy Rain. S.W. Wind. 11 am. 14 D. 6/130gs 2 reinforcements. Visits X" & new Staff.	
	27		Mild bright. L'Keny arrives L.Keny admin N.A.C. General Routine etc.	
	28		S.W.Wind. very shiny during day. Visits new Staff. General Routine etc.	
	29		Clear. Mild. 72 reinforcements from Base. 33 for Infy. 3 9th RH. Visits X" General Rankin's	General Rankin
	30		Heavy Rain. B.Q.M.S. Pte Lewis from Base. General Rankin etc.	
	31		Heavy Rain. L'Chalmers proceeds to our Divy and visit Xn Brigadier Phillips. General Routine etc.	

R.Daly Leech Lt.Col
Cmdt 2.D.A.C.

2ND DIVISION
DIVISIONAL ARTY.

DIVISIONAL AMMUNITION COLUMN.

R.F.A.

JAN - DEC 1918

2nd Divisional Artillery.

2nd DIVISIONAL AMMUNITION COLUMN R.F.A.

JANUARY 1918.

WAR DIARY or INTELLIGENCE SUMMARY

Army Form C. 2118.

2nd D.A.C.

Vol. II
Jany. 1918.

Place	Date	Hour	Summary of Events and Information	Remarks and references to Appendices
Hazlewood	Jany 1st		Col. Shing Weed. Proceeded with S.C.R.A & Convoy to new position.	General Routine etc.
	2		Mid. Mickp. all Bgds. Buses to return by 1 & 2nd 6.A.R.P. 28779 9th Lyzgerald	
			Aid currying eight 1 & 2nd Post Mickp. to be held. Visits X'd General Routine etc.	
	3		Brig Beng L. 1 Opl. 14 ORs enclosing T.M. Mat. Capt. OBrien L. Warker proceeding	
			Rouen Sealing Bty. Base for instructional Purpose.	General Routine etc.
	4		Col. Others & L.P. Bali returns by Officer. 17th Div at Corps Dump. 1 Sey & 190R	
			to Cops & Dumps. 6 Ores enqolis at Rail. Visits X'd enclosing bomb proof walls.	
			arrives ex Slabbo. General Routine etc.	General Routine etc.
	5		Col. + Adj. 2nd Bali: & R.A. Corps Handeclogue. Material to New Slabs	arvid-
	6		Clear. Col. Capt. Meade returns from Leave. Visits New Slabs. General Routine etc.	
	7		Rain overnight. C.O. 1 O.R. gains from Base. Visits H.Q.R.A. General Routine etc.	
	8		Shing S.S. Wind. Revs. BSM Woods to Hospital. 1 S.Wagon hired & Dunin 6 Left Div. Wing.	
			for Newton Arch. 1 Opl. 1 OR gains from Base. General Routine etc.	
	9		Col. + Clear. Move to Condoy cancelled owing to Slab. Road. General Routine etc.	
	10		Rain overnight. 4 6.2D arrives from Base. General Routine etc.	
	11		Shing Weid. S.E. 4 6.R.D. Chobetocher 9. 36. Bgde. 21. 41st Bgde. 2 D.A.C. 6.2 Wago.	
			Returns from Corps H.A. General Routine etc.	

WAR DIARY / INTELLIGENCE SUMMARY

Army Form C. 2118.

Vol. II 2nd D.A.C.
Aug 1918

Place	Date	Hour	Summary of Events and Information	Remarks and references to Appendices
Hopsheuvel	Aug/8 12		Very cold. Wet-cloudy. Visits X's. Work carried on in Stables. General Routine etc	
	13		Milder - Clear. Visited RAHQ. General Routine etc.	
	14		Misty. Capt H Roberts M Proceeded on leave 8 days End. Visits Med Staff. H.Q. Lieu Q.H.Q. General Routine etc	
	15		Rain. Strong Wind S.E. 1.15? O.R. from Base. General Routine etc.	
	16		Rain. Strong Wind S. 2/Lt Graham, 6.71°.15°.16. 16-37 E.Y. Statlis. 1 S.S. Reinforcements, Joined from Base. General Routine etc.	
	17		Rain during day. Capt Cook 2/Lt Chalmers returned from leave. Visits X. General Routine etc	
	18		Cloudy, 4 Raining Latterly. 6.M91xb Visits Siths General Routine etc.	
	19		Misty Cloudy. 4 G° 6 Siz Say. T.M. Crews. General Routine etc"	
	20		Misty Cloudy, 1 G° - 18 O.R. W Dept. B ungone Bn 2/Lt Gong 4 Many if 75 men leaving etc at TRECULT	
	21		2/Lt T P Raylay ... Joined ... now from England 2/Lt Tony Ward ??? ... OR also in charge of all Army Mess.	

WAR DIARY
INTELLIGENCE SUMMARY.
(Erase heading not required.)

Army Form C. 2118.

Place	Date	Hour	Summary of Events and Information	Remarks and references to Appendices
Mullacoot	22		Services day 14.6.1 lay the emergency date ready to go Regiment at Doreinet & composite Police from Bur No 31ST Fairly indifferent day the Gen Richards Capt 2nd York & Lancs Tk un ARP here	
"	23		63rd Div actions 2nd F/heward Sett 4 No 4.16 Inf attacked 2nd E.T. T.M.S. 2nd ET Captured went in to lines 2nd E.Y 4 WA have been well of reinforce and they Bur Cultury and more Pub is Yeoman 2 of Pierce	
"	24		Juni & Bur – ventire	
"	25		Artillery actively on 2 Bur – ventire – including 6 Bur – ventire	
"	26		Artillery actively on unchanged they have any 7 (concent one) left in our S 2 Coys rifles Coys 2nd F Ray in Sing Bing in rear returned from rest Coys by Signed will Ventery	

WAR DIARY
INTELLIGENCE SUMMARY
(Erase heading not required.)

Army Form C. 2118.

Place	Date	Hour	Summary of Events and Information	Remarks and references to Appendices
Hesmond aux 27th			Fine day. Flight & 2 Lieuts Munby & Curtis NCOs & men marched from the Divisional to Etaples Sinclair & 3 Lieut Drummond & 2nd Lieut Leary proceeded on leave. 2nd Lieut Drummond & 2nd Lieut Liell returned from leave. Lieut Lockley Bus Offr & Capt Byrne	
Fute	28th		Fine — 2nd Lieut Liston returned by 2 Bg outlying lines into billets.	
			Fine — not good air startups for flying	
	29th		Mid-night day. Returned to S. Legare & 5TH Vincent	
			— returned —	
	30th		Fine troops by markers provided Stable up ARD	
			Flight Lieut Newton wood on leave — 9 men posted to TM5 Fine place new Establishment — W/S 2625/76. J.C. FLANELL	
			T on rig accidentally by a fund at ARD Remounts	
			hospital	
	31st		Wet & Fine day — Capt J.C. Potato returned from leave	
			2nd Lieut W.S.J. Caine proceeded on returning leave to Yorkville	
			J.P. Byrne Capt RFA	
			July 3rd DAC	

2nd Divisional Artillery.

2nd DIVISIONAL AMMUNITION COLUMN R.F.A. ::

FEBRUARY 1918.

WAR DIARY or INTELLIGENCE SUMMARY

Army Form C. 2118.

Vol II 2nd D.A.P. Feby 1918

M 43

Place	Date	Hour	Summary of Events and Information	Remarks and references to Appendices
Corley	2/1/8 1st		Sharp frost. Helio live telephone apparatus. See showing photo. panel radio etc.	
	2		Col. & Lieut. L. & 3 visited field 6.17 & Bty 60R & 7th Bde Sigs. Pte Jagger	
			Sgt I Reeve. Lines. knowledge. Pt Bate & 38R from hons. course	
	3		Pt Pawton on course from 3rd Army Battery School. General Routine etc.	
			Friedrich Corp. 16th M.E.C. Corps D.D. Coup Exercises by Pawton	
	4		Officer. General Routine etc.	Heavy
			R.D. Training. Repairing. Haulage. Snowing away trenches etc.	snow
	5		Service light apparatus. C.H. 2nd Ou nob live. Pt Rhodes Jamieson	
			base. Repairing. Van Stay etc. General Routine.	
	6		Eve'd. Car Sy. ZZ Kaudof Colt 5 TNS 10.0R 6t PH H 5th	
			Capt Hackforth returned from leave. General routine etc.	
	7		Dull & showery. Col Kelly & L Clunie Vauban. 2W Buoy exercise L. Gaus	
			Sorm 6630 L Sgt Peake accents. E.S.H physical. general routine etc	
	8		L Clunie J.D. Jamieson Bee.	
	9		Fine & bright showing. Sharp. General Routine etc.	
	10		Fine & bright. Helplacement. Lappels Check, Dover. 4343 BSM	

WAR DIARY or INTELLIGENCE SUMMARY

Army Form C. 2118.

2nd D.W.R. Vol II Feby 1918

(Erase heading not required.)

Place	Date	Hour	Summary of Events and Information	Remarks and references to Appendices
Corbie	2/8			
	10		34343 13 S.W. Terrans Jons from 88/B Oge 2LD Kens 3 LD wounds. Every shell Spnio. Genrnl Routine etc.	
	11		Lieut MCQ & L.P.S. Church Service transfer LtCol-Provid rev days. Sear Recruits. General Routine etc.	
	12		Lieut Elm. Capt Reyt Procd to Corr 10 days 6 Eng Leave. General Routine etc.	
	13		Light Kens 34 "B" A wounds & hit up killed Entry L. Power actions from tely. Corr Abeville. General Routine etc.	
	14		Lieut Obur. 2/L Keyes Q.R. Joins from Base. 2/L S.H. Woods. 2/L Olive vrou L/lt. Musketry. 13/G 2/L. F. Keny returns from Corr. General Routine etc. Practice 20 OR from "X" 1st & 2nd V.R.Q.	
	15		Lieut other. 2/Lt Atwell & S.H.A." 20 R to Range Musketry Practice for 1st & 2nd . Owning of the now General Routine etc. Foot Drill & other exercises.	
	16		2nd Other. Lt Muskly Practice at Range. Foot Drill & rifle exercises in afternoon. General Routine etc.	
	17		C.O. Other 10 R Jons from Base. 2/L M Stevens Jons from Base. Weapons Church Parade. (Lieut W. White E6.	

WAR DIARY or **INTELLIGENCE SUMMARY**

Vol II 2nd DHQ July 1918

Army Form C. 2118.

Place	Date	Hour	Summary of Events and Information	Remarks and references to Appendices
Kohat	18		Lieut & Class Musketry Practices at Range. 1st D.A.H. Rifle exercise. General Routine etc.	in Office
	19		Lieut Class R.H. Bay & 52 DR Gous from Gen Musketry Practice. Reph.	
			Sharmi & Foot Arms. General Routine etc.	
	20		Lieut Range firing Officers. 373 B.S.M. Rgr. passed 1st form 81 '15 Std.	
			2nd Class firing from Guns Musketry Practice. Foot Drill Rifle exercises.	
			General Routine etc.	
	21		Lieut class 1 Sq & 100 R attacks A.K.P. 21 Mepds organis from N.C.A.	
			21 O Tring pulrouds or Cer. 300 Gun Snows tun Musketry Practice.	
			Foot Drill & Rifle exercise. General Routine etc.	
	22		Lieut Class. 1.2.2 classes General & Annals attacks S.P.S.	
			Musketry Practice. Foot Drill etc. General Routine.	
	23		Lieut Class. Musketry Practice. Foot Drill Rifle exercise. General Routine.	
	24		Lieut Class 2nd Weigh VR #19 Rt Gun from No. 373 16 S.P.B. Gunners	
			W. & exeen. G. 16 "15 Std. Inspected Church Parade. General Routine etc.	
	25		Raining. General Routine.	

Army Form C. 2118.

WAR DIARY
or
INTELLIGENCE SUMMARY.
(Erase heading not required.)

Vol II 2" SHC
Feby, 1918

Instructions regarding War Diaries and Intelligence Summaries are contained in F. S. Regs., Part II. and the Staff Manual respectively. Title pages will be prepared in manuscript.

Place	Date	Hour	Summary of Events and Information	Remarks and references to Appendices
	Feb.			
Calais	26		Shops Work. Chr. 220K. b- B Offrs reinforcements.	Musketry Parker Post
			Drill. CO proceeds Etaircourt inspects 7R.2 SHAX + Wayam	
			1st 2nd Reinforcts. Arrange as at lasting days ab Guinchaux	26
			M.O. Cheestp. Musketry Bayonet Stlelton Driving Drill	Post Daire etc.
	27		R.P. Both Advance from river	L.W.K. Weigh attack 5.8.9K.
			General Cautious.	
			B.Hy.	
	28		Recce Class S. CO orders Bentification Musical	General Gubbins Etc

2nd Divisional Artillery.

2nd DIVISIONAL AMMUNITION COLUMN R.F.A.

MARCH 1918

WAR DIARY or **INTELLIGENCE SUMMARY.**
(Erase heading not required.)

Vol II 2nd D.A.C. Army Form C. 2118.
March 1918

Place	Date	Hour	Summary of Events and Information	Remarks and references to Appendices
Corbie	1st		Cloudy. Showers during day. Officers & Ours. [Rowers] 1 & 2 & 3rd & 4th Sq. 6. H.Q. General 6. Clock and overhaul stores etc. with wagons there. Musketry Practice. Rowing. Driving. Foot Drill. B.Q.M.S. Clark joins from 6th Div. General Routine etc.	
	2		Persisting. Very cold & windy. 2/P.S.Q. Capt. Atherton & 47. & 15/13. 2nd E. & B. Queens joins from time to Works 6.48 & 15/13. Musketry Practice. Rowing. Driving & Stores & Bus. Drill. Routine by the Section. Horse management debit N.C.Os. General Routine etc.	
	3		Raining. Very Cold. 2 Gunners joins from Base. R.Sergt. Rowing Dis. General Routine etc.	
	4		Fine. 1 S.D. evacuated 6 to U.S. Musketry Practice Rowing. Driving & Foot Drill. General Routine etc.	
	5		Fine & clear. Lt. Beton approved 2P.A.A. from Musketry Practice Rowing & Driving & Foot Drill. General Routine etc.	
	6		Fair and mild. Musketry Practice. Rowing. Driving. Foot Drill. General Routine etc.	
	7		Fine & clear. 5 D & 40 auxs. GNo.5 Workers Bdy. R.O.F. 10 Sta. occur forward 6.15 & 15/13. D.H.Q. & 2 Coys. 6.17 D. moves No. 6 D.C.S. Musketry Practice. Rowing. Driving. Foot Drill. General Routine etc.	

WAR DIARY
or
INTELLIGENCE SUMMARY.

Vol II 2nd DAC

March 1918

Army Form C. 2118.

(Erase heading not required.)

Instructions regarding War Diaries and Intelligence Summaries are contained in F.S. Regs., Part II. and the Staff Manual respectively. Title pages will be prepared in manuscript.

Place	Date March	Hour	Summary of Events and Information	Remarks and references to Appendices
Corbie	8		Fine rather cold. Personnel on 14 days leave 2/Lt Duncan 24. 6.93 AFA Bde.	
			Long Range Musketry Practice continued. Posting Diary. 2nd Lt. General Markin att. Fort Dill Bye School.	
	9		Fine rather cold. 2/Lt 94 Bry SR & H. His reports from Milo Cove Rifly School.	
			2 G.S. Wagon attached ARP Column to Shelter. Long range Musketry Practice. Posting Diary.	
			Fort Dill General Markin att.	
	10		Fine rather RE CODE parade. Posting Diary Fort Dill. General Markin att.	
	11		Fine rather cold. S.T.M. 36 +41 "Bdg supervising. 2Dr 5.41 "Bdg.	
			10.D. 6 ARP replace Bonnell. 16 G & 2Dr. joined from Base 1 Rank & NCO.	
			Musketry Practice Ready & Dinn Div. General Markin att.	
	12		Fine work. 16 G. 2. 6. Bdg a reinforcement. 2Lt 94 How 6.170 Hy. 2Lt 94 BySm 6.93 Hy.	
			Musketry Practice Ready Dinn Div. General Markin att.	
	13		Fine rather. HQ 1 + 2 Xth Wind from Guilay 6. Filly Sais Cobie. General Markin att.	
			Fine rather.	
Ville sur Corbie	14		Fine rather. Arriving here Bligh att. General Markin et.	
	15		Fine very cold. 115th 133 3.D. 10 miles. 6. No.5 ARP workeny Pty relieving No.4.	
			Attached. I will I. 18D. 24 miles. 6 ARP. 6. Relieve Saunder Paty. Attack Fire	
			Corp. 173 Bocent 1147. Naser Personnel joined from Reserve. 2nd Galloway S.I. + 2 L.	
			J.O Woos 14 days leave Bagdes. General Kaplan et.	

A6945 Wt. W11422/M1160 350,000 12/16 D. D. & L. Forms/C./2118/14

WAR DIARY
or
INTELLIGENCE SUMMARY.

Vol II 2 D.H.Q. March 1918.

Army Form C. 2118.

Place	Date	Hour	Summary of Events and Information	Remarks and references to Appendices
Villa Sin Cubri	16		Line talk. G.O.C. Ladder. Flagg & Capt. attached to 63 Div. repairing Park Battery.	
			Ridney & driving Div. Russian Reserve. 121 Gun. + 10 Squadron Sandjerm	
	17		Base No 950565 G Avres. absent from own draft. Rept Trans at Cam. General Routine etc.	
	18		Line at Warm. R.E. New Bn. Church Parade. General Routine etc.	Routine General
			Line & clear. 89 G. - 6- 63 Div. Ridney & Driving Drill. Russian Reserve.	
	19		Maury. 2/L. W. Chalker L. Harrel 7 Russkan U15 eulu + 22 Dr. Jones from 13 Sz.	
			88 g. reads 63 Div. reports 6-2 R.A. altd 6-36 & 6-15 sz. 39 & 16 Sq no 20.	
			feels to 36" - 41 S. 15sqe. General Routine etc.	
	20		Clear J. & Cy. Cshaw. Kidney Drill. Indian Reserve. General Routine etc.	
	21		Line at early. Preparing for wear to Bazentin to R.H.	
	22		Line. Grows 1 - 2 x "57F10 6- Bazentin le Petit. Arranging Camps etc.	
Bazentin	23		Line Clear 25 Kms east from 11 - 28° - 21 H.Q. 6. Stationer area 6 Bass 6.12.1815 + 5. 15	
			Ishural. Vogan. General Routine etc.	
	24		Bay M.O. Ben N.I.X Clitches R up "B.51" 47 Div N° 2 X " £ 36.15.93 old 6.1 Pharsel 11.30 6.	

WAR DIARY
or
INTELLIGENCE SUMMARY.

Army Form C. 2118.

Vol II 2nd DFA
March 1917

Place	Date	Hour	Summary of Events and Information	Remarks and references to Appendices
Rumilly	25		Divisional HQ. Received 12 wounded men at 5.P.M. See Rev. officers dug out in General	
			vicinity of 2nd Div.	
			R.H. proceeded to see Lieurance	Capt. Mars & Lords to L Albert & Inspection of RH
			No 1 & 3 Gas on Nelson Road	Glasgow was Ken L Strevens
			visit to Boden	No 2 L Bailey-Isabel both in lines
	26		Boyd Leca Revd Gones Steward to Vrecetile	visit L.M. to RA.R. forward
			2" R.H at Berlincourt apered	R.H.A. 3 SW. Rev. Even to mess to Albert
			Found up with No 2 & 3 SRH.	No 1 & 3 march from Steurant to Cohuite.
Achiet	27		Can Hr. No 2 & 3 S.A.R. went to Inurni	Rev. Rest No 1 & 3 Vaucourse
	28		G.O. Deny P.W. Wing. King Gerrard	
	29		Raining 247 M.B. Personel attached to evd. D.O. 1 & 2 K.	for duty with orders to take over
			2166 " & 145 How Gerald 36 " rd " Bdes Wheeler Received Row Ron Bdes. marching	
			Gen. C. 27/26 Corps go Forward.	
	30		Lieut. 190 R. revisits 3 Tha ? Arranged with R.G.U. Often Col. Debred 6 oct (with 1 Troop	
	31		Raining L. Defro & Stoff Visit av Dumps 9 AM Cohuist. 1st & Bdes relief Gen. C	
			6.30 om arr. Achiet	Geolyn J.L. Col 2. DFA

2nd Divisional Artillery.

2nd DIVISIONAL AMMUNITION COLUMN R.F.A.

APRIL 1918.

Army Form C. 2118.

WAR DIARY
or
INTELLIGENCE SUMMARY.
(Erase heading not required.)

Vol II
April 1918

2nd D.A.C.

Vol 45

Place	Date	Hour	Summary of Events and Information	Remarks and references to Appendices
Vervins	April 1st		Fine & clear. 69 Gun & 34 S" Posts 6: 36 sel: 1st Bgds. P.S.W. Back returns from leave	
			6 Eng. Ewas. 22 S.D. Galliwat 28 S.Woods returns from leave & Eng as. @Pachis	
			Wagon. stores Etc. Genl. Routine.	
	2		A.C.W. Cloudy. 30 O.R. per A.S.T. 36" 69sch" 153ch". 75" L.D. from Pickvillers.	
			23. 6. 36". & 52. 6. 41". 153ch". R. 2 Meschan fieeds. 636 DB"g. N° 291354 S. 1st Lieutenant	
			6 Hospital Wounds. Genl. Routine Etc.	
	3		Dull light shower. N° 2 X "B" Wagon unloaded from 1st 36 "Bgds Wagon Lines.	
			10 S.D. Bgd a reinforcements on leaving Wagons & Transport. General Routine.	
	4		Heavy rain. KANO unit & Pickvillers. 2nd Detn. landed on ARC Pichart £63 Div	
			Genl. Routine Etc.	
	5		Clear & fin. Co. Wir: H.Q. 1st 2 X. D.A.C. & 2nd Thn. 3rd Marches from Vervins	
			21 L.D. Reinforcs. arrived from Pickvillers.	
Milly	6		Mild & clear. Rain during night. H.Q. 1st 2 X "DH. & Tn 3rd Marches to Bellevert.	
Bellevert	7		Fine & clear. 21 S. D. Reinforcs. 6 S.D.A.C. Cpl. Berin arriving 1st on leave Lent Routine etc.	
	8		Rain & cold. 3 O.R. 6 The 3rd. I. Chalk. 6/z Ten 15th. 1st 15 cents. 6 1/2 Tim 15th. 1st Lieut. 6. A. 36.	
			3 L.D. wounds. 6 VMS. Genl. Routine etc.	

A6945 Wt. W14422/M1160 350,000 12/16 D. D. & L. Forms/C/2118/14.

WAR DIARY or INTELLIGENCE SUMMARY

Army Form C. 2118.

Vol II 2 ORC
April 1918

Place	Date	Hour	Summary of Events and Information	Remarks and references to Appendices
Guidecourt	9th		Rain. C.O. HQ 1st X 2nd Marchd to Reg. Camped outside of village c/o of Shelling	
	10		Cloudy. Res. 3 N.E.S. 5 O.R. joins from 150au. Genl Kavtine L	
	11		Fine clear. HA 1st X 2nd Marchd S. Yucayasar X?	
Mazagon	12		Fine clear. L'loeks. 1 N.E.O. 16 O.R. Strench Dump. Pt Balw. Nest. Cyphous 6 Tml	
			L't finile cops 1st Go Offrs R.A. Genl Kartine eli.	
	13		Cloudy. 1 N.E.O. 10 O.R. 6.1 ODAC Dump. Sabin. L't Ploise joins from L Cpl Genl Kartine	
	14		Cloudy tooldwind. 20 reinsmen. 2D arms from tea. L't Ploise arrived L't bike at	
			New Lee dump. Sapents less 1st & 2nd inshicken resum 6 more losse eur. 7 Feb	
			Struck prov. Genl Kartine eli.	(Cogline)
	15		Cloudy & Cold wind. 20 LD Kemerls refrects by Cp L Barler with mdons 6 BOHc Pars L	
	16		Cloudy rains. 2 K'Smel Alack L 713 1/2. Sey Sale A V.C. joind from 14 W.S. Kasfeh	
			Genl Kartine eli	
	17		Cloudy fine. L'loeks Alack 6 47 15 1/2. Genl Kartine eli	
	18		Very Cloudy by Grau. 1 N.C. 10 O.R. joins by 1 ODAC of logsic fring L. Genl Kartine	
	19		C.O. L't Thompson Alacks 6 D36. 6 Sudan recrnbonenls joins. 1-15th San Offseks from	
			No 1 Gun B.R. Genl Kartine eli	

Army Form C. 2118.

WAR DIARY
or
INTELLIGENCE SUMMARY.

Vol II 1918 2ⁿᵈ D.A.P.C

(Erase heading not required.)

Instructions regarding War Diaries and Intelligence Summaries are contained in F. S. Regs., Part II. and the Staff Manual respectively. Title pages will be prepared in manuscript.

Place	Date	Hour	Summary of Events and Information	Remarks and references to Appendices
Wadajen	20		Fine Day Ch. Arab 1ᵒ2Xᵒ ATAQ. General Routine etc.	
	21		Fine Chor. 2 Officers 2 N.Cos from 1ᵒ2Xᵒ b-accounts + county Tour. CRO inspects Line. Genᶫ Routine etc.	
	22		Fine clear. Enemy aircraft on Zug district. Genᶫ Routine etc.	
	23		Clear 3 Miles P. Shirell took 6 M.Learn Dumps from Pentah Dump. Genᶫ Routine etc.	
	24		Clear misl. 21 Arn report from 17/13th. P.M.Bath 5-11/13th L.P.Victoria 5-15/13. Genᶫ Routine etc.	
			Inspects 1ᵒ2Xᵒ ATAQ. Genᶫ Routine etc.	
	25		Clear 3 miles. L.Ricket 6-47/13th L.Hawthorne 6-71°/13th Genᶫ Routine etc.	
	26		Col. Sten G.J. 30 gᵐ x 22 Dᵒ reinforcements from Base. Col. Routine etc.	
	27		Cloud 3 miles. Party from Mel'Jean Camp. (return). Genᶫ Routine etc.	
	28		Very much (cold). Genᶫ Routine etc.	
	29		Stormy Rain & cold. 1ᵒ Patrick Evening. Lts Lower Slater Shanley from for inspection Zᵒ x Tanks. Major Lyth and Capt E. McIntosh from Base. Genᶫ Routine etc.	
	30		Clear 3. Col. recounting their Arrick + feed to Base returned. Genᶫ Routine etc.	
				Clive Alphan Lt Col. AD 2DAC

A6945 Wt. W14142/M1160 350,000 12/16 D. D. & L. Forms/C./2118/14.

2nd Divisional Artillery.

2nd DIVISIONAL AMMUNITION COLUMN R.F.A.

M A Y   1918.

WAR DIARY
or
INTELLIGENCE SUMMARY

Vol II
May 1918

2nd D.A.C.

Army Form C. 2118.

Place	Date	Hour	Summary of Events and Information	Remarks and references to Appendices
Suzanne	May 1		Nothing to state. Windy. Capt. McBain to Command of D.A.C. Vice Lieut. General Routine etc.	
	2		Fine clear & windy. 1st D.A.C. on taking over A.T. 2/Lt Brewath & x 2 N.C.O. 15 Men. General Routine etc.	
	3		10 O.R. rec'd 1st D.A.C. Palais & occupied at Cachew Dumps. 2 Lts. Service from "Burg" Rifles. Camps. General Routine etc.	
			Fine & warm. Country hard, water & forage scarce. 2 Fitters attached to 1st Bde.	
			No 35/20 9. Working in "No 1/A" Park, wounded at H.Q. of L.F. wagon attached to N.W.S. General Routine etc.	
	4		Fine & windy. Visited 1st D.A.C. Brigages taking over A.T.T. for 3rd General Routine etc.	
	5		Showery & Dull. Took on A.T. from 1st D.A.C. Ammunition & 2nd L.H.A.T.T. L'Horses.	
	6		Served from 64th Bde. A.F.A. General Routine etc. Fired & Clear. 2/Lt. Hodges attached to 17th Bde. Sgt. Quigley crowns Sgt. Lewis of Duty. 2/Lt. Hawthorne attached from 71st "Bde" attached R.P.P.K.B. General Routine etc. No "1 x".	
	7		Heavy & rainy during morning. N.D. 1 x Z.A. wounded / wir rendezvous No. 5 Corner. 6th Rendezvous amm'd & R.P.Wagon att'd. This making a total of 5". 1 N.C.O. & 7 O.R. from 71st "Bde". Having completed fatigue. Parading 60 P. Clouds. Firing. Steam Lew. M. Belch. No. General Routine etc.	
Gouves.	8		Fine & Clear. "1st / Lt. Pr. Ook. b 71st" B'n on attack by over # Hugunt. 6.9" Hobson. 6.17" Gunn. 4.71768.13 " 2.	

Vol II
WAR DIARY
or
INTELLIGENCE SUMMARY
(Erase heading not required.)

Army Form C. 2118.

2nd D.A.R?

May 1918

Place	Date	Hour	Summary of Events and Information	Remarks and references to Appendices
Souves	9	a.m.	Fine & clear. 8ICB "72 L.D. joins from base. 1 Waiter & 3 Sudanis S.O. join from base. General routine etc.	
	10		Cloudy, bursts. 8No. 72 L.D. inspected by Capt. Webb, and distributed 6.13 sqdn. & S.R.P. Genl. Rtn. etc.	
	11		Fine & clear. Field Day. H.Q. 1 & 2 X? practice P.type.5 Am 1st 6.13 sqdn. Men in afore.	
	12		Fine & clear. 5 S. & 9 O.R. 6.13 sqd. as reinforcements. 1 N.C.O. & 6 O.R. attached L.T.M.S fatigues.	
			N° 40145. Pte. Stone S. wounded. Genl. Routine etc.	
	13		Slight rain cloudy. 6 Sudanis join from Base as reinforcements. Genl. Routine etc.	
	14		Fine & clear. Pte. Daniel Sweeny. 8? Burmar. Wds. wounded at A.R.P. Sr. Debrev 10tres	
			on A.R.P. Genl. Routine etc.	
	15		Fine very warm. H.Q. transferred North Marsh. Genl. Routine etc.	
	16		Fine & clear. 2/Lt. Gepp 6.17. 1/13 Bn. 2/Lt. Lucas 6.47. Lewis Routine etc.	
	17		Fine & clear. P.S. Lipton in hosp. with hernia. & 2/Lt. Hampton & SNAA x? C.R.A. infirmary	
			2/Lt. Lucas. Genl. Routine etc.	
	18		Fine & clear. Inspection L.R. Bty. automobiles. Genl. Routine etc.	
	19		Fine & clear. Genl. Routine etc.	
	20		Fine & clear. Visits R.H.A. 1 & 2 X? 1st Rank March, with Roscommon march. Genl. Routine etc	

Vol II

WAR DIARY
or
INTELLIGENCE SUMMARY. 2nd A.H.P.
(Erase heading not required.)

Army Form C. 2118.

Instructions regarding War Diaries and Intelligence Summaries are contained in F. S. Regs., Part II. and the Staff Manual respectively. Title pages will be prepared in manuscript.

Place	Date 1918	Hour	Summary of Events and Information	Remarks and references to Appendices
Gonars.	21		Situation. Quiet Day. H.Q. 1st 2nd X" Corps. Aust. Surps & recong. workers.	
	21		Col. 2.0.P.W.R. visit on Gen'l S.P.A.H. L" Koester. Gen'l Radini etc.	
	22		Situation. N° 224 S.B. Hosp'l L" Eppey. Lamed from @19.15 de. 17 m Div. Gen'l 2 Rostino etc.	
	23		Situation. 6 Russian R" Newport near Base. R" Kooney f"day wounded. 1 Mule Kebs. N° 2 X"	
	24		Raining. Cold rawish. Gen'l Rostino etc.	
	25		Situation. Cap'n W.B. xxx Mayorus N° 1 X" 1 Cpl. Rdh. 2 S.S. 13 Gor. 12 Dm. for info on Base.	
			24" Fld 6 Hospital (?) (visited by emb). Gen'l Rostino etc.	
	26		Situation. L' break expects 6 S.P.Q 11. ? XVIII Cetera for emers. Fard Rostino etc.	
	27		Situation. S' Cashern & temp address. Funds warrant of am'l' Lyftr. 1 Cpl L"Ho 2 SS. 8 Por.	
			12 D.r. 6 P"39's. Gen'l Rostino etc.	
	28		Situation. 1 S.g. 1 P". 10 Gen'r 4 D' from Base. North lived H.D. 1st 2 X".	
	29		Cemetry. Gen'l Rostino etc.	
	30		Situation. 1 NCy. 1.1" OR. expect. 4.8.6.37. Cath. talgas. 2/Lt' Wilson joining from H.D.P.O.	
	31		Situation. Gen'l Rostino etc.	

Godolly Lt Col
Comdg 2nd A.H.P.

2nd Divisional Artillery.

2nd DIVISIONAL AMMUNITION COLUMN R.F.A.

JUNE 1918.

WAR DIARY
INTELLIGENCE SUMMARY

Vol II 2nd D.H.Q. June 1918

Place	Date	Hour	Summary of Events and Information	Remarks and references to Appendices
Govro.	June 1.		Fine & Clear. 18 P.O. & 5 Pvts. & exchanged at A.R.P. by 1+2 X. Sey "Cultural Perets 6."	
	2		N.A.H.R. as Sr. NCOs. Gen'l Routine etc.	
	3		Fine & Warm. Church Parade. Gen'l Routine etc.	
	4		Fine & Clear. S.O.R.H. ea.w.d. General Routine etc.	
	5		Fine & Cloudy. 2 POWs returning of Auth. drawn from A.R.P. by 1+2 X. Gas Parade. General Routine etc.	
	6		Fine & Clear. Inspection 1+2 X 3 with V.O. General Routine etc.	
	7		Fine & Clear. Routine Parades. Box Rep.& Parade. Gen. at Rowhis etc.	
	8		Fine & Clear. General Routine etc.	
	9		Fine & Clear. Visit Dentist. General Routine etc.	
	10		Cloudy - cooler. General Routine etc. 10 g & 10 Pr 6 b& 41"1590. Reinforcement.	
	11		Dusk - cooler. Inspected X 1+2. Gen'l Routine etc.	
			Fine & Clear. 10 O.R. 6 Theraanne T.M. School 2 Drawn from N°1 X & N°2 X.	
			2 ODuty from S.A.A 6 N°2. 2/4 Review 6 S.A.R. from N°1 X. Gen'l Toulouse 6.	
	12		Fine & Clear. 8 g & 1 S.S. joined from "Army Rein." Camp. L. Drewen 6. 47"/5157. Gen'l Routine etc.	

Army Form C.2118.

WAR DIARY
INTELLIGENCE SUMMARY

Vol II 2nd D.A.C June 1918

Army Form C. 2118.

Place	Date 1918	Hour	Summary of Events and Information	Remarks and references to Appendices
Gouves	June 13		Fine. Clear. Genl Routine etc.	
	14		Cloudy. 166743. 2nd Lt. J. Hare. 8.30 a.m. Nerve's. Genl Routine etc.	
	15		Clear Fine. 2/Lt Hawkis. forwd from X 567N. 188 from Base. Genl Routine etc.	
	16		Cloudy. Light showers in morning. 2/Lt Howell & 1 Army Schr. Labour Party Cadre	
			Coying. fine pm. visits 1st & 2nd. Genl Routine etc.	
	17		Cool. Lt Moorie during day. E.S. Wagons return from Blys. & Q.S return	
			with 7th 13thy. Genl Routine etc.	
	18		Raining. Arranged with 15th D.A.C. re handing over Dumps A.R.P. 17 & 18 of same	
			from base. away a/c landed 65 T.M. Returned. Genl Routine etc	
	19		Dull & Windy. Rain during evening. [crossed out] Genl Routine etc.	
			1st Cmd Cyclone from XVII 1st Corps Remps. Genl Routine etc.	
	20		Cloudy. Light rain. Genl Routine etc.	
	21		Cloudy. Handed over A.R.P. to 15th D.A.C. Genl Routine etc.	
	22		Strong Wind & Cloudy. Move from Gouves. at 7 A.M. carried Gouves experience	
			12 noon. took over line from 40th D.A.C.	
Gouderson	23		Clear. Fine. L. Farm forwd from base. took over S. Aman's A.R.P.	

WAR DIARY or **INTELLIGENCE SUMMARY.** 2ⁿᵈ D.A.C.

Army Form C. 2118.

Vol II June 1918

Place	Date	Hour	Summary of Events and Information	Remarks and references to Appendices
Saudrupt	1918 June 23		from 40 K.A.C. Genl Routine etc	
	24		Cloudy. Sudan Showers from bar. visits S.A.A. 1st & 2nd Genl Routine	
	25		Fine clear. Capt McLean wounded on 19th. Major Johnston bar. visits H.Q.R.A. Genl Routine etc	
	26		Fine clear. 6 O.R. attacks 6 T.M.B. visits (gunnery) H.Q. C.R.A. on Zinnes from 31st D.A.C. Lt Wolaby 6- N.2X from N.01. P.M. Chang Lt Revis 6-15 R.H.Ly. Genl Routine etc	
	27		Fair clear. Visits H.Q.R.A. P. Ross will attacks 6-17 (13) Bty. Genl Routine	
	28		Fair clear. 27h Whitson 6- G.O. Course. 3rd Army School. Visits S.A.A. 1st & 2nd Genl Routine etc	
	29		Fine clear. 2 Lieu etc. D. Govin from bar. Genl Routine etc	
	30		Fine clear. Hailcoln Major Nislan Pugh 6- Kaw. 15 D & 26 D & Col. B.D. to Genl Routine. Major Naslin Pugh 6- new estab hvaut. L. Kuschy (form.)	
			Reinforcements 41 O.R. 6- Bode Suf 6- new estab hvaut L. Kuschy (form.)	
			from bar. P. Kurso 6- G.O. Course. VI Corp. Genl Routine etc.	

GoDalziel Lt Col
Comd 2ⁿᵈ D.A.C.

2nd Divisional Artillery.
———

2nd DIVISIONAL AMMUNITION COLUMN R.F.A.

JULY 1918.

2nd Divisional Artillery

No. B.M.

Instructions regarding War Diaries and Intelligence Summaries are contained in F.S. Regs., Part II. and the Staff Manual respectively. Title pages will be prepared in manuscript.

WAR DIARY or INTELLIGENCE SUMMARY
(Erase heading not required.)

Vol VII   2nd D.A.   Army Form C.2118.

July 1918

Place	Date	Hour	Summary of Events and Information	Remarks and references to Appendices
Quderewjon	July 1st		True & clear. No 3081 G. Lindow L. Sig b & No 33815 Shaumer trans.d to Engineers Loco to 6th b. Hospital. Visits A.R.P. S.A.A. X & A.R.P. Genl Routine etc.	
	2		True & clear. L. Presselt arr.d from 1st Army on School & charge evacuated Stn U.S. Visits No 1 & 2 Stn Genl Routine etc.	
	3		Dull & hazy. L. Freeman Chas Stinson & G. Jones from 3rd Army "Reinforn" Camps. Sgt Lawson b. R.H. Newton Hospital as G.M.Sgt. Genl Routine etc.	
	4		Clear & fine. C.R.A. inspects 1,2 & S.A.A.X. L. Welch returned from Rein 6 Eng Dr. General Routine etc.	
	5		True & clear. Gunner Burrow Gr. Goins from Rein No 965747 Gr Shimes L. Weeks b. 1.R.H.Q. as Sanitary orderly. Genl Routine etc.	
	6		True & clear. Gnr Dotson & Wilkes & Corpy Rence 3rd Army Corps School L. Kirches & Young from P.O.Camp Lt. Wilson b. Hospital. L.D. evacuates 6 M/S Genl Routine etc. Visits A.R.P. (Gunner & G'can).	
	7		True return 11 O.R. Joined from Rein Corp. L. Puney Warren b.Ga. Crease. Genl Routine etc.	
	8		Cloudy. #32 L.D. Reinforcements from Rein depots b.V.O. & Archibald b.Fb.Dep. D.A.C.	

A6945 Wt W1422/M160 350000 12/16 D.D. & L. Forms/C.2118/14.

Army Form C. 2118.

WAR DIARY
or
INTELLIGENCE SUMMARY.
(Erase heading not required.)

Vol. II 2nd D.A.C.
Feb. 1918.

Instructions regarding War Diaries and Intelligence Summaries are contained in F.S. Regs., Part II. and the Staff Manual respectively. Title pages will be prepared in manuscript.

Place	Date	Hour	Summary of Events and Information	Remarks and references to Appendices
Grandrieux	Feb. 9		Showery. Fine Officer showery. Inspected Anzac at Rowlin RE Dumps Div. orders	
			Nails + tapes publish for ARP use. Appx's 6. Red. effect SCR A. Lt. Corah L. Lewis Gas Gun.	
			Genl. Routine etc.	
	10		Fine. Cloudy + showers Afternoon. 6 Guns of B/ 6·36. Bde. 3pm. 6OR. Cpl. O'R. Bde. 4. go 6 T.M.	
			Angus events. Lg Lewis from ARP. Cpl. Ritchie to G-ARP. visits ARP. Genl. Rout	
	11		Fine. Raw Army Afternoon. 3 OR G ARP. 3 Hrs. pass G forw from Base. 1 LG plus	
			No 1 X" Visits No 1 + 2 X" Genl. Routine etc	
	12		Raining 189". 2 OR G. 6·36" Bde (fatigues) Cpl. Hill To RA advd. Depot for exams in Sadans	
			Language. Cpl. Mc Lean returned from leave. L. Wor(e)sley from No 2 X" G. No 1 X" Visits PA?	
			1a. Genl. Routine etc.	
	13		Cloudy. 3 N.CO's 3 OR G. 2nd Div. Gas course fitting eye pieces etc. O'Lewis from RA	
			Aleutian Hospital S. Award. Genl Routine etc.	
	14		Fine. 1 each ARP. Lt. Corah from Gas Course 15" Benson G. Lewis Gun Course	
			Genl. Routine etc.	
	15		Cloudy very close. 6 P.S. 1 Lt. Lt. 1 P.S. G. 3/15 Bde. 12 P.S. S. Signallers 1 Lt. from	
			Base. 3" Army Riefer sent Course. 13 QMS. Clark G. 175" A.P.A.13. on promotion G. 13 SM.	

A6945 Wt. W14422/M160 350,000 12/16 D.D. & L. Forms/C./2118/14.

WAR DIARY or INTELLIGENCE SUMMARY

Army Form C.2118.

Vol II 2ⁿᵈ D.A.P. Feby 1918

Place	Date	Hour	Summary of Events and Information	Remarks and references to Appendices
Quesnoy	Feby 15		Sgt Padley from 153ʳᵈ A.F.A.Bde. to N° 2 X⁺ on B.Q.M.S. Genl Routine etc.	
	16		Heavy rain & Sy'acle feets 6. 17 Bde. L.t Kirchin 6. 41° 1:30 p.m. 1 O.r. & 26 Dis Jones from Divs DAC to 2 L.D. evacuate 6. M.V.S. Visits DAA. Y.	
	17		Fine & showery & Sigwallen feets 6. T.M.3. 18 Grs. Joining Divs. 3ʳᵈ Army Reinforced Camp. Genl Ryle.	
	18		Physl. Showes during Day. 2" L.t M. Kellow adm'd to Hospital. Visits. N° 1+2X⁺. Genl Ryle.	
	19		Fine etc. 10 OR 6. T.M. Course. 2ⁿᵈ Army School. L. Monroe 6. 13 O.R. 6. Bbs. visits per Remounts. Visits A.R.P. + H.Q.R.A. Genl Routine etc.	
	20		Fine, very warm During Day. L. Ellerby & England subject 6. Sig Reunion by Divs transpr. 6. R.A.F. L.t Woloby. 20. O.R. 6. Norville. 6 ended Desville Rail. exchange 6. A.R.P. 1 LD evacuate 6. M.V.S. Genl Routine etc.	
	21		Dull+Burdy. AR Ryle inspects by A.O.C. 13 endeavs. to overrides L. Kennedy. Spots. returns from Athies with Arowents. I Miller 6 M.V.S. Visit D.A.A. Genl Routine etc.	
	22		Fine + very clear. 3 Ors 6 13 Dis reinforcements. Capt. Hawthorne 6 England on leave. Genl Stoughton 6 La Crosse 15" Bren. adming gen. Lewis gun Course Visits. A.R.P. L.t McKay attends. 6. D. 36 Bde. L. Ritch 6. 17.", L. Fowke 6.16". Genl Routine etc.	

WAR DIARY or INTELLIGENCE SUMMARY

Army Form C. 2118.

Vol II 2nd D.A.C.
July, 1918

Place	Date	Hour	Summary of Events and Information	Remarks and references to Appendices
Gouzeaucourt	July 23		Raining. L/Cpl Welch L/Hook report to 2/c R.A. Douthwaite for 1 month course A.A.	
			John Coates Gagan 2nd D.A.C. L. Duncan joined from 41st Bgde. 1 Rft. joined from 3rd	
			M.V.S. feralis 6 S.A.A. Visits N.1 & 2 X" Genl Routine etc.	
	24		Fine. Warm. 3 L.D. called by D.A.C. 3rd Army. L/Cpl McGee to Hospital. Accidentally ill.	
			sick. Genl Routine etc.	
	25		Fine. Very warm. Cpl Eckersley Hospital G. A/170 Bgde R.F.A. 6 Pm. 75" S.I Grey	
			Joined from Base. Visits SAA X" Genl Routine etc	
	26.		Heavy rain during night. Showing during day. Visits A.R.P. Cpl Hogg this afternoon/2 am	
			Gas course. Cpl Pluigh for duty with Div Cartier. Genl Routine etc	
	27		Raining. 3 N.Co. & 37 O.R. eng to Fatigue 47'/15 Hq. Genl Routine etc.	
	28		Fair but cloudy. 3 N.C.S.Ty. 37 O.R. eng U. Fatigue 47'/15 Hq. 163231 Pnt Vail W.H.L. wounded	
			@ 12.6. Hospital. Visits N.1 & 2 X" Genl Routine etc	
	29		Fine. 6.9.15 from Base. 15" Dodson & G. Whitaker ayourpour country Chees. L/Laurie from 2.6.15 am	
			S. occurain no 2 X". 13 ORs Pack By. G. A/151 Bk. Genl Routine etc	
	30		Fine. 11 OR 6.36" 18 OR 6.41" of 6 OR G. T.M. Newport. Sergt "Kerry" from Base p.1.6.36". Cpl "Werth" Supp 2	
				"forms"
	31.		Fine. 6 Sig B & St 15" & 6 Sig E 1 OR from one. 10 OR 6 T.M. R.S.M. course 14 days. Isaac & Say Cd. Paid Rte Stk	
			Godley Lt Col. Comdt 2 D.A.C.	

2nd Divisional Artillery.

2nd DIVISIONAL AMMUNITION COLUMN R.F.A.

AUGUST 1918.

WAR DIARY / INTELLIGENCE SUMMARY

Vol II August 1918 2nd D.A.C.

Army Form C.2118.

Place	Date	Hour	Summary of Events and Information	Remarks and references to Appendices
Gouchenpré	1918 Aug 1		Fine weather. 2 Sudan OR joins from Res. 5 S.P. Wagons rec'n.	B & Z Coy
			R.E. daily fatigue, lectures. Draw: 1 P.D. his SRA IN Co 11 OR attached to 4th Bde. Vehicles, Wbgs, & Bang Dumps. Gen'l Routine etc.	
	2		Showery. Reinforcements 6.36 th Bde. 1 NCO 24 OR rejoined from 38th Bde. Vehicles SRAI's. Gen'l Routine etc.	
	3		Showery. Pt Gen'l Sir E.J. Scott inspects Sudan Brownie D.A.O. N°4716.81 P.O. Were joined by Lieut by him. Wagon passing O & him. Vehicles N°4/4 Z.4th Gen'l Routine etc.	
	4		Fine clear. Cpt Sh. Norton org. 6.16th S.Vy. Cl 21 Bde. 4.5 OR rejoined at H.Q. Actions & labor units 2.3 OR D.A.O & Bde SRA? 1 NCO 11 OR rgn 4th Bde polign. Gen'l Routine etc.	
	5		Lig & anin. 3 Cy gallops juched 6th The'l Vehicles HRP Gen'l Routine etc.	
	6		Showery. 2 OR 6 3rd Army New Camps. 6t OR occup. Crumuls Junifores Bois 1 OR L 6 Corps Cookery School. Gen'l Routine etc.	
	7		Fine weather. Washer & OR 6 Abbeville for remounts Cp. to Hor. Noris returning from love 6 days. Gen'l Routine etc.	

WAR DIARY
INTELLIGENCE SUMMARY

Vol II
August 1918

Army Form C. 2118.

Place	Date	Hour	Summary of Events and Information	Remarks and references to Appendices
Gasanjam	Aug 8		Lieut Colonel J.D. Evanochi Transferred SAH & 2B Ord Shell time	No 28.
			Lieut Stockforth 6 Hospital Diatis AMP. Genl Kowlin etc.	
	9		Lieut Colonel 6 M. & 36th 13 Bde 3 OR 6 AKP, vide 1 & 2X.3 2nd Sect alm	
			Returned with 6 Kanowlis wound 6 OMP. Genl Kowlin etc.	
	10		Lieut Colonel visit PAH X". Genl Kowlin etc.	
	11		Lieut Colonel KPM Burwell 13 Bty Lieut Jn. Sup. Taylor Capt 15 Bde	6.
			Engineers for trip of Irrum Irvine — Genl Kowlin etc.	
	12		Lieut Colonel 9 OR 6 The & 8 OR 6 36th 13 Bde 2 5 OR 6 41° 13 Bde 9 Sup W Tyler	
			Serves from tour L'Craph Cawah. ('Eng Caird). Genl Kowlin etc.	
	13		Lieut Colonel visits AMP. Genl Kowlin etc.	
	14		Lieut Colonel Capt 20 Meade 6 England 10 days Comm. Genl Kowlin etc.	
	15		Lieut Colonel 10 OR 6 AMP 2 DB 6 M.U.S. 4" Currency Jones from turn 10 OR	
			Rejoining from Turn o Genl Kowlin etc.	
	16		Lieut Colonel 1 Fr. Sept 1. Z. S.S. Jones from tour. 6 OR returns from 36° 13 Bde.	
			Visits AMP. Genl Kowlin etc.	
	17		Lieut Colonel 2nd Wood Sup 1 Kelly 6 Anty Class. 3rd Army A School. Genl Howlin.	
			6 Engineers report for duty. Cadet School. Genl Kowlin etc.	

Army Form C. 2118.

WAR DIARY
or
INTELLIGENCE SUMMARY.

Vol II 2nd D.R.P.

(Erase heading not required.)

August 1918

Place	Date	Hour	Summary of Events and Information	Remarks and references to Appendices
Gauwespen	18		Cloudy & dull. 3 L.D. 6ºU.S. Clind. Visits HAX & NºZ. Genl Kentur etc	
	19		Fine & clear. Visits H.Q. Genl Kentur etc.	
	20		Dull & cloudy. Gen Goldworthy stard. 6.3ª Army near camp Visits HKP. 1 Officer 40 O.R. from 3 Div Rgt 6. Whigs Troops trainy. 15 O.R. aus personnel from Base. Genl Kentur etc.	
	21		Heavy mist. Cloudy. Whigs & Bang Troops Lowestro 6. 3rd Div. L' Morris Ginshow Base. Visits Co 3 Div. Genl Carkwell	
	22		Fine & clear. Visits RAH.Q. 1 P.S.B. Gunshow tree. Genl Kentur etc.	
	23		Fine & clear. SHAX tire 6. Brewillie Co. Wagon Nº 23. Stokes& Nº Appendix 13etc. tire on Whigs Bang & Nermery from oun Dumps from 3.D.M. Visits RAHKP Genl Kentur etc	
	24		Dull, robust. Visits HKP established main Dumps et Durby. Genl Kentur etc	
	25		Fine & clear. Visits Whigs Bang Nermery Stacks Dumps. HRP. Gun Kentur etc.	
	26		Fine & clear. Forward dumps established Corvells. KO. 1 & 2 & 7ª D.R.P. moves from Gauwespen to Mouely. 3 L.D. 5 U.S. Gt Genl Kentur etc.	

Army Form C. 2118.

WAR DIARY
or
INTELLIGENCE SUMMARY.
(Erase heading not required.)

Vol II 2 W.R.R.

Month: August 1918

Place	Date	Hour	Summary of Events and Information	Remarks and references to Appendices
Noordy	Aug. 27		Few relov. All G.S Wagon 1/2 X & W/Ds Salving Am: from Sachs Qun	
			firalini. Visits A.P.M.S. 15 OR from 1 Base reinforcements #B301 L/Hogan J	
			22 500 5 L.Davis wounds + 20 w/os to Hospital. 1 L.D. Wounds:- Rifl. J Briggs	
	28		N.C. Scouts from tree. Cred. Ratine eb.	
			Dull showery. All G.P. Wagon Salving. Visits A.P.M.S. N.O.I.C.A. G.W.Colview eb.	
	29		Few relov. A.P.D 1/2 X more 6-6 Owing Rain. 2/" Wesly Strauch	
			Rocks AA 15 Hz. 1 L.D. S.Afr. S. Chind. N° 6671 S Expl. Wrush 1 other.	
			9 G.S Wlls 6 L.D. Recruits Wounds. Cred. Ratine eb.	
	30		Fine rbov. 7 OR 6 36 "Bge. 130R 641/Bgde. Expl. Marshaw. Ross Cpl. Pack	
			11 Ogrs from Bose. E.S Wagon Salving Am. Visits A.P.C.C. Cred Ratine eb.	
	31		Cpl Williams 15 T.W. attacks D.H.Q Salving. 1 OR 109 Nem astrd M.P.P. from	
			62 Div. G S Wagon Salving. Cred Ratine eb.	

G.A Hopps / Lt Col
O Cmdg 2 W.R.R

2nd Divisional Artillery.

2nd DIVISIONAL AMMUNITION COLUMN R.F.A.

SEPTEMBER 1918.

WAR DIARY or INTELLIGENCE SUMMARY

Army Form C. 2118.

Vol II 2nd D.A.C. Sept. 1918

Place	Date	Hour	Summary of Events and Information	Remarks and references to Appendices
Pr. Queevy Farm	1918 Sept 1		Lieut Evans Acting Adjutant. Capt. S.W. Briggs M.C. trans. to 63 Div. Visits HHQr G Section, S Group. 2nd Divn. Vans & Gen Reskins. Gen T Rorkeu &c.	
	2		Div Cher SAH X" move from Re Queevy Farm to Founcourt 68179 D'invest 6. Hospital. Gen'l Rorkeu &c.	
Ercheu	3		By Dr. moves forward. HQ 1+2X" move to Ercheu. All Batteries Ercheu. Advance All Established at Founcourt 49106 B.S.W. Artic from 16"18"57 fruits. 6 N"1X". 23 LD arrvd from Bernies. Batches 36 Brigade 8+ 5-1"5 Fo. Bledge & Fresnoy. etc. batches from THI. 6 N"2X". Gen'l Rorkeu &c.	
	4		Div Cher HQ N"1+2X" moved to Ercheu. All Batteries at Vrais Wapen Bns. B centred. 14 D" Wagon 11-25" M trays by Camp Plenfic. Gen'l Rorkeu &c.	
Vauscaup	5		Div & Cher & Askarken Bingham & Essen 1708. Ro. S. Lrs. b. Rispalles. Accidently wounded by front. 1 LD N"1X" Bounds by foun wounds 6 (MVO) (Visits HHQr) Gen'l Rorkeu &c.	
	6		Div & Cher 13 Cn, Arz 5" Wagon relieve 6 SD. Chair lin will Bgde Arts N" 1+2X". Gen'l Rorkeu &c.	

WAR DIARY or **INTELLIGENCE SUMMARY**
(Erase heading not required.)

Army Form C. 2118.

Vol II
Sept 1918
2nd D.H.Q

Place	Date	Hour	Summary of Events and Information	Remarks and references to Appendices
	1918			
Thessaloniki	7		Fair & fine. 34.2 & 43.13 S.M. Survey. 6 Eng. how Orders & 38 Fd Amb Sr.	
			or course. 185" & 93" fwd from base. No 131787 S. Seymour Kiosk Shelter.	
			96764. D. S. Bream wounded & adm. Hospital. 3 L.D. Rein. L.D. wounds by bomb shell.	
			Lt. E. 13 Cavalry adm. 6 Hospital. L.P. Wagon taking Rns from 6 th Lieu Division.	
			Gen Kortine etc.	
	8		Fine. Sky wind E.W & rain. Visited H.R.P. 4 & 5 L.D. from base. 36" Bde S.A.A.	
			25. St. P. & 10. 4 L.D. & M.T. S. 1 L.D. killed shellfire. Railway Rne to Lt Kortine etc.	
	9		Wet. Sky W & W & fair. 16 O.R. & 36" Bde Reinforcements. 34. O.R. & 4L D Reinforcements.	
			Salving Ammn. Gen Kortine etc.	
	10		Cloudy by O.G Showers. Visited H.R.P. Gen Kortine etc.	
	11		Showery cold Sd Wind. Gen Kortine etc.	
	12		" " " 24.O.R. from base, tons, reinforcements. L. Dept. Bengal.	
			Spent Leave. F.P. Wagon salving Rns from 6 t Div. Gen Kortine. Visit N.R.P.	
			Gen O Kortine etc.	
	13		Good. Lt Theuser 6 C.R.P. Visits H.R.P. 1 x 2 x " Fd Kortine etc.	
	14		Fine rain. All Wagons salving. L. Wilson reports from Hospital. Gen Kortine etc.	

WAR DIARY
or
INTELLIGENCE SUMMARY.
(Erase heading not required.)

Vol. II 2nd D.A.C.
Sept. 1918

Army Form C 2118.

Place	Date	Hour	Summary of Events and Information	Remarks and references to Appendices
Bertrand	15		Fine & clear. All Coln arrived from Exelmes & Communes Étangs. 6. 93.6. Battery Course.	
			Gen'l Routine etc.	
	16		Fine & clear. 14°C-6.36". 13 Bde. -S.O.S. 6.y. & W. Hampton sent to. 3 L Bns. Lours	
			& advanced 10M. 25.33. 1 Corpl. & 20 L.Dr. Joined & were sent to camp, etc. from base.	
			Gen'l Routine etc. Arranged with S.C.R.A. Reinforcement Dump.	
	17		Fine & clear. Heavy shower as soon & rain early morning. 9th Div. F.P. coop A.R.P.	
			2 Killed & 3 W.M. Sick. New face value.	
	18.		Fine & clear. 2/6 Col. Sucheart on Case & 2/Lt. J. Badger & 2/Lt. J. Parker	
			Met. New Regt. attached to us. Stores etc. 40 Bicycles.	
			collected & whole column on the 19 on 2 Rows. Bde 26, A.H.Q., U.G.D.A.C. 6.	
	19		Fine & clear. 2/Lt. Paris (Corby Febford) & Nault went to Corps	
	20		Army to Paris proceeded on case & Parish Could squire as a Corpl	
			20 Pers. 6 y. 2" T.M.B. etc. arriving at Infantry Yd picture	
	21		Fine & clear. 15 Prob. enlisted in D.A.C. allowing Men in full.	
	22		Fine. clear. 24 Reinforcements sent to Bijensy. 4.4.16. from to Coldet	
			Adelbert to Jfeller. 36 Brigade 20.2. Brigade 20.7. D.A.C. 4.	

WAR DIARY
or
INTELLIGENCE SUMMARY.
(Erase heading not required.)

Army Form C 2118.

Place	Date	Hour	Summary of Events and Information	Remarks and references to Appendices
Sept 1916	22		September. 1/5 2 NCOs & 10 Gun. detail from Base H/Q arrived. Pte Sanders returned from Cert.	
	23		Very [illeg] class. 1/5 49th Bde returned to Group (routine)	
	24		Very clear. 2/25 F. [illeg] wounded, admitted 5 N.F. Cly Nantilles. Mud & Russ. Bnr returned to 1/5 B. 25 Inst. 3 Indian order noted	
	25		Obs. Bnr.	
			Rain in morning. Cleared up later. 2/ Reinforcement Bnr H. Bon	
			Reinforcements joined by Div-Sess-NCOs (routine)	
	26		Fine & clear. Capt. Ridley. Inspected all Guns & Vehicles to 3/ B. & H. on 6/ (routine)	
	27		Very clear. Very misty 2 writing supplied from H. Vincent H. Warnicourt,	
			Aust. Clair started at F.I.B. at 0 a.m. & art by VI Wing. Main Maury 5 [illeg] (routine)	
	28		6/ returned and J. Pace Jack. VIII. (routine)	
			Very clear. [illeg] tended lorry & truck returned to dump whilst 2/ M. Mc Tire	
	29		Mist in morning. 23 Reinforcements to Bde (routine)	
	30		Dull and misty. V.N.Cs 1 & 2 visiting went to width of [illeg]	
			and [illeg] & [illeg] carried out to 6/ W. Note 1 L.O. delivered by	
			Memory Cpl. (routine)	

Pt Barker Cpl
2/Lt QAC R.F.A 30-9-16

2nd Divisional Artillery.

2nd DIVISIONAL AMMUNITION COLUMN R.F.A.

OCTOBER 1918.

Vol II October 1918 WAR DIARY 2nd D.A.C. Army Form C. 2118.
or
INTELLIGENCE SUMMARY.
(Erase heading not required.)

Place	Date	Hour	Summary of Events and Information	Remarks and references to Appendices
Huwawoofs	1		Finished Cst & Officers Mess & 2 Subs recovering on location for lines Wess Mess Word Genl routine etc.	
	2		For Obar. Newly RANKS NT 1 & 2 N.C.Os & one to Oriel Wood 2nd Farm returns from Divisione Genl routine etc.	
Oriel Wood	3		Five relief Off Establisher at 4.11 & 37. 4 OK Jours from no. 1 Res & 74 S Five relief Off. Revolished at 6.11 a 5.7. 2 AM Wayne damaged at same times. Killed. 2 LD Wounded by enemy Shell fire. Genl. routine etc.	
	4		Puie O. Am. Bombing Coops. Duier. Interestig. And New Varhi Southery. Genl Routine etc.	
	5		Five class. 3 Indian NCOs to hew Artillery College South. 74 Westhams C. 46 19th 17 Gunners Rear Rieg Londow to DAC Camp Baptisis Eivie Park Athenaeun. N. Park, Cal Gun End Gun 11 OR Depot Depot sent of Eng. from 5 LD of D.A.C.	
	6		Draft of men from Base (hay Cand) 2nd Delay ran from to Engd. 2 Doc ones of Officers from Italy nos3565) 1 grade a3fi G hospitals wound. Beg. Rev him. Puie Plan.	
	7		Am forecow Storm Charon. 3 off sig & Bordies 5 1 a R to. Distinguish Celly Gun X Ca Struck out Wounded. Cong. Shell fire 5 1 a Wounded. 3 of lost came to Engd. 3 2 received at Infantry as followers. 36 20 41 of 7 D.A.C. sent Cashui etc.	

Vol II

WAR DIARY
or
INTELLIGENCE SUMMARY.
(Erase heading not required.)

Army Form C. 2118.

October 1918   2nd D.A.C.

Place	Date	Hour	Summary of Events and Information	Remarks and references to Appendices
Overloon	1918 8		About 65 drains found THIRD line Ration etc	
	9		Practice. Guard RH took on Guard of 8th SMQ went to RHIR Gen	
			Routine etc.	
	10		Practice. 320 men. 10 8MGS went on. 100 R.M.D.	
			Cloudy. Bry change, change day. RD 1st 2nd SBC went SB Weather	
Hoevels	12		Heavy clouds. Rain shower. Sept. 1 Sept 19 OC from troops took parts	
			across the 40 R. 3 men wounded by Capt Walker Lieut.	
			Genl Routine etc	
	13		Dull etc. 8 OR recruits came Capt Hilly + Colour Sergt Cunningham	
			Practice Preview shoot tried the shots of 13th NCOs holes in 36th	
			SDC 6. Salvage Burl + loading case 6 MGS Genl Routine etc	
	14		Fine robrain 150 bat. 6, 36th + 10 ORs 41st Bdg. H Stevens wounded etc	
			etc. Gen Routine etc	
	15.		Cloudy. No 640501 1st OR SL.K Cavalry @ 30 473 Bg Lifed +	
			Cord from Base Street 36th 5030. 55 OR Jan'y Base Gen Routine etc	
	16		Raining. 4 Sudan OR joined from base. 1 choge 6 MGS. Gen Routine etc	

WAR DIARY
or
INTELLIGENCE SUMMARY.

Army Form C. 2118.

Vol II 2nd D.R.P.

October 1918

Place	Date	Hour	Summary of Events and Information	Remarks and references to Appendices
Mogetto	17		Cloudy. 19 OR & 36 other ranks 41 Bde & 41st Bde as reinforcements. Solway line from Vocks Gen Zeit. A.R.P. established at O 30 Central. Genl Routine etc.	
	18		Strong wind, wearing Sr. officers. HQ 1 & X move from Mogetto to Fairoaks. 10 Sigs and 15 OR joined from base. 2/Lt Johnson joined from base, posted to 41 Bde. Genl Routine etc.	
Fairoaks	19		Cloudy. 1 NCO & 40 OR from Reg'tl Camp. Joined the Allard Ctr. & 1/Lt S Vaud. Genl Routine etc.	
	20		Raining. 6 Sigs and 2 OR. 36th Bde. 4 Sigs and 2 Wheelers Nobs to 41st Bde. 220 OR US. Genl Routine etc.	
	21		Dull. Light Rain. 2/Lt Cunning shrink of Strength Bund. Palsang. Rue to 14 B & 14 US. Genl Routine etc.	
	22		Raining. HQ 1 & X march to St Vaud. Genl Routine etc.	
St Vaud	23		Very cloudy. Established A.R.P. at V 24 Central. Violin NACH and Routine etc.	
	24		Fine clear. HQ 1 & X march to St Lyphon released to APM W.9.6.37. 2/Lt Mowbray joins from Base posted to 36th Bde. 2/Lt Gilliam rejoined etc. England 14 days leave. Genl Routine etc.	

WAR DIARY or INTELLIGENCE SUMMARY

Vol II   2nd D.A.C.   October 1918   Army Form C. 2118.

Place	Date	Hour	Summary of Events and Information	Remarks and references to Appendices
St Hylier	25		Fine morning day. By U. Rain evening. Lt Duncan returns from Paris leave. Lt Bolston Eng. U.S. wSpecial 18 OR rejoin unit from base. Visits H.Q.R.A. Genl Kerluin etc.	
	26		Fine & clear. Saluting Am 'A' & disturbing O.O. in 6 A.C.A. Genl Kerluin etc.	
	27		Fine morning afternoon rain during afternoon. Capt Mason Dsw/24 6 W9037. Capt Mahon evacuated wounds in leg. 27 O.R. 6.75gd & recruits in re-enforcements 1 O.R. from base. 2/Lt Burgess Eng. Am joins. Genl Kerluin etc.	
	28		Fine clear. Saluting Am 'A' disturbing Dame 6 W9637. 3 D.A.C. late arr from 2nd D.A.C. under orders of 3 D.A. Genl Kerluin etc.	
	29		Fine & clear. 2nd D.A.C. late arr from 3 D.A.C. C.R.A. visits Unit. 3 L.D. from U.S. Genl Kerluin etc.	
	30		Fine. visits H.Q.R.A. Genl Kerluin etc.	
	31		Raining. Sg P. Kellog 6 Hospital Sick N° 81777. D. Thompson killed in W. Europe Sh/L1 1 Rd, & from U.S. visits H.Q.R.A. Genl Kerluin etc.	

Ayhouse ?
Lt Col 2 D.A.C.

2nd Divisional Artillery.

2nd DIVISIONAL AMMUNITION COLUMN R.F.A.

VNOVEMBER 1918.

WAR DIARY / INTELLIGENCE SUMMARY

Vol II   2/w S.T.C.   Nov 6 1918   Army Form C. 2118.

Vol 52

Place	Date	Hour	Summary of Events and Information	Remarks and references to Appendices
St Cyprien	Nov 1		Fine, clear. 13 B.O. 6 Sur. Reinforcements from Trou. pour. R. Mopeer	
	2		Going from base No 1336 S.T. Bus. Stopped at N4 S.T.T.D. 1st & 2nd Dull, light rain. 40 L.S. Reinforcements arrived. Q.S. Wagon carries our rations tor. Pat. at 15t. Gen. l. Karluie etc.	up " Col. Pat " Sav Pat
	3		Dull, light rain. S.T.A.C. and 2 Quo. S.T.A. from 10 A.M.	Salling Aue.
	4		Fine. No 1 + 2 X" now 6. Reserves. 10 9" + 12 S" to B.Co. Reserve. 1 S.B. (No 2 X" Coad) 1 Res. (No 1 X") killed by Shell fire. Gen. Korluie etc.	
	5		Raining. H.O S.T.A.C. moves to 6 Reserve. Col. M. Mayflower leit 6 Laglish.	
Reserve	6		14 days leave. Gen. Korluie.	
	7		Raising. Threats 1 + 2 X" Salling Aue. Gen. Korluie etc. Cloudy & rain. 2 nd Broch + Ramble. Relieves S.T. our Caur. reg (Pass) Salling Aue. Gen. Korluie etc.	
	8		Close & rain. No 1 X" moves to Reant. au Sant. L.T. Law + 41 D.T. Reinforcements to 2 L.S.R Wounded. 6 N.C.O.S. Salling Creeke Geo. R Korluie etc.	
	9		Fine. No 2 X" moves to Reant au Sant. No 1 X" 6. Ridgeres Col. Korluie	

WAR DIARY or INTELLIGENCE SUMMARY

Vol II 2ⁿᵈ D.H.Q. Nov 1918 Army Form C. 2118

Place	Date	Hour	Summary of Events and Information	Remarks and references to Appendices
	Nov			
Roodia	10		Div. H.Q. D.H.Q. moved to Freins Col. 1ˢᵗ S.A.I. Bde to 6.36. ⁴ᵗʰ Bde. S.A.H.A & M.G. Bn from Esschau & 6 ᵛⁱˡˡ B? Genl Roulers etc.	
	11		Div. Ceasefire 11 A.M.	
	12		Div. 40 O.R. 6ᵗʰ Bgde reinforcements. 2ˢᵗ L.D. 2 Bn. 6 M.G.S. Genl Roulers	
	13		Div. 1ˢᵗ S.A.I. Bn returns from line to Esychut. Genl Roulers etc.	
	14		Div. M.Q. D.H.Q. S.A.H.A. Lⁿ moved & Audignies. 2ᵗ Warwick & Genl Roulers etc	
			65 O.R. reinforcements. arr. from line	
Audignies	15		Div. 36 O.R. reinforcements. 6ᵗʰ Bgde. 7 L.D. 6 M.G.S. Genl Roulers	
	16		Div. 70 L.D. troops removed. arr. from line. 5 O.R. from 15 13/g	
			Genl Roulers etc.	
	17		Div. 5 S.P. Wagons horses & men 6.36 ⁴ᵗʰ Bgde. 4 S.P. Wagon horses & men 69?	
			2ⁿᵈ S.A. Buck 6. Com? No 2 X. Genl Roulers etc.	
	18		Div. Officers Riding. Genl Routine	
	19		Clear 7. 70 O.R. reinforcements Joins Div Reinforcement Camps. Genl Roulers	
	20		Div. Col'n Marches from Audignies 6 Maubeuge. Col Roulers	
Maubeuge	21		Div. halts at Maubeuge fatigues in lines & on roads. Genl Roulers etc.	

Vol II 2ⁿᵈ D.A.C.

Army Form C. 2118.

WAR DIARY
or
INTELLIGENCE SUMMARY.

Nov. 1918

Place	Date	Hour	Summary of Events and Information	Remarks and references to Appendices
Maubeuge	Nov. 22		Fine + bright. Halt at Maubeuge. Fatigues in town + records. Lieut. Belgain Interpret: L. Von Bock M. joined for duty. 3 Lucien McGowan from France. Genl Routine etc	
	23.		Fine + Frosty. Halt at Maubeuge. Capt O'Brien returned from leave to England. Genl Fatigues etc.	
	24		Fine + Frosty. D.A.C. March from Maubeuge to Lebeau. Col. Vol. arriving 1.30 P.M. Genl Routine etc	
Estines Val. 25			Cloudy. Slight rain. D.A.C. marched to Fontaine le Veque arriving 4 P.M. Genl Routine etc	
Fontaine Le Veque 26			Cloudy. Halt at Fontaine le Veque. Fatigues in town. Genl Routine etc	
	27.		Dull + stormy. Genl fatigues in town. Genl Routine etc.	
	28		Raining. Halt at Fontaine L. V. Fatigues in town. Genl Routine etc.	
	29		Fine. D.A.C. moved from Fontaine le V to Avesnes arrive 2 P.M. Genl Routine	
Avesnes 30			Fine. Halt at Avesnes. Genl Fatigues in town etc.	

G.D. Algernoth
Col.
Cmdg. 2 D.A.C.

2nd Divisional Artillery.

2nd DIVISIONAL AMMUNITION COLUMN R.F.A.

DECEMBER 1918.

Vol II

WAR DIARY
or
INTELLIGENCE SUMMARY

Army Form C. 2118.

2ⁿᵈ O.K.R.

December 1918

53

Place	Date	Hour	Summary of Events and Information	Remarks and references to Appendices
Oiseau	Dec 1		Fine noon. C.R.A. visits lines. P.S.C. part direct off Shimpl Cushioly. W.O. Col.	
	2		A.G.40. A/201/18. Gen'l Routine etc.	
	3		Fine. Gen'l Routine etc.	
	4		Cloudy, rain during day. L'Mafele. 10 O'R. 6 Names. 6blush Removals. Gen'l Routine.	
	5		Raining. D.H.Q. march from Oiseau to Lewis. Arriving Lewis 1-30 P.M. Gen'l Routine etc.	
Lewis	6		Fine. D.A.C. march from Lewis to Thou Samson. Arriving Thou Samson 1-20 P.M. Rts.	
	7		2ⁿᵈ L. Gulling proceeds 12.12.18 days leave England.	
	8		Fine. D.H.Q. march from Thou Samson to A.H.N. arriving A.H.N. 12:30 P.M. - Rts.	
	9		Fine. D.H.Q. march from A.H.N. to Perry arriving Perry 2:30 P.M. Gen'l Routine.	
	10		Fine. D.H.Q. march from Perry to Aywaille arriving Aywaille 2 P.M. Rts.	
	11		Fine. D.H.Q. march from Aywaille to Grand Co arriving Grand Co 2:50 P.M. Auto.	
	12		Rain during day. Rests at Grand Co. Gen'l Routine. C/o	
	13		Raining. D.H.Q. march from Grand Co to Thervmont. Arriving 1-15 P.M. Cross-roads (German) Capt. O.E.C. Meade thrown from his horse wounded 6 64 C.C.S.	
	14		Raining. D.H.Q. march from Thervmont to Budge lock. arriving Budge lock 1-30 P.M. Gen'l Routine etc.	
			Gr. Sgt I.H.A. X. New O/S by Capt. Curry. evacuals 6 C.C.S. Gen'l Routine etc.	

Army Form C. 2118.

WAR DIARY
or
INTELLIGENCE SUMMARY.
(Erase heading not required.)

2nd D.F.A.
Vol II
Dec 1918

Place	Date	Hour	Summary of Events and Information	Remarks and references to Appendices
Bulgersloof	13		Wet. Saw marched from Bulgersloof to Kalkkloof arriving 3.0 pm	Genl Kokin etc
Kalkkloof	14		Raining. Review day. DHQ marched from Kalkkloof to Kollsbroch arriving 2.30 PM	
Kollsbroch	15		Raining. Rests at Kollsbroch. Genl Korbin etc	
	16		Raining. Rests at Kollsbroch. Genl Korbin etc	
	17		Raining. Rests at Kollsbroch. Genl Korbin etc	
	18		Raining. DHQ marches from Kollsbroch to Lenders dorf arriving 2.30 PM	Genl Kokin
Lenders- dorf	19		Showers. Rests at LENDERS DORFF. 4 Indian R. Inns from Boer	Genl Korbin etc
	20		Fine. DHQ marches from Lenders dorf to Burks dorf arriving noon	Genl Kodenis
Burks-dorf	21		Fine. Arrival day. Settling + allotting billets. Staff etc	Genl Kokin
	22		Raining. Col. + Capt. Forsl attended HQ RA (Educational scheme) 2 weeks	6
	23		August 14 days leave Raining. Capt. Forsl being end of returning as Educational boards Korbin etc	Genl
	24		Fine. Getting Lewis into shape. Genl Korbin etc	
	25		Holi. Fine. 50 OR Reinforcements from Boer. Genl Korbin etc	
	26		Fine. Rain during afternoon C.R.A inspects Lewis fields DHQ	Genl Korbin etc

WAR DIARY or INTELLIGENCE SUMMARY

Army Form C. 2118.

2nd D.H.Q.

Vol II
Dec 1918

Place	Date	Hour	Summary of Events and Information	Remarks and references to Appendices
Düsseldorf	27		Raining. 44 O.R. 6.34.36 + 41 ot Bdes. Genl Routine etc.	
	28		Raining. R.N.C.O. Course from Base. 20 O.R. 6 England. 18 Cos ümm + 2 Pistols Demobilized. Capt L. Shaw Hames (England). On leave. Genl Routine etc.	
	29		Raining. 15 O.R. 6 England. 14 Cos ümm. 1 R. Seven War Rumbly 2. Genl Routine	
	30		Fine. 10 O.R. 6 England. Demobilized. Genl Routine etc.	
	31		Fine. 4 O.R. 6 Walford Battn for duty. Genl Routine etc.	

www.ingramcontent.com/pod-product-compliance
Lightning Source LLC
Chambersburg PA
CBHW080904230426
43664CB00016B/2720